T0325486

Praise for Leading with Character

"As leaders, we choose how we show up. No matter what level you are, never forget that others are watching. We model behaviors for people around us, setting expectations for how we expect to be treated and what we expect of others. This defines the character others see in you and takes courage. Always be authentic, and if you are your best in the ordinary moments of life, you will be great in the extraordinary ones."

—**Cathy Engelbert**, Commissioner, WNBA, retired Deloitte CEO

"I've been extremely fortunate to have worked with Dr. Loehr over several years. His program has been invaluable in helping me grow personally and professionally. As a leader, I want to bring my very best at home and at work. We are all chasing something, as Dr. Loehr so clearly points out, but what really matters is the impact of that chase on our character. Through his teachings, I now understand how to strengthen my muscles of character so I can be the best version of myself in every aspect of my life."

—**Billy Donovan**, Head Coach, NBA Oklahoma City Thunder

LEADING

WITH

CHARACTER

ALSO BY JIM LOEHR

Mental Toughness Training for Sports
Breathe In, Breathe Out
Toughness Training for Life
The New Toughness Training for Sports
Stress for Success
The Power of Full Engagement
The Power of Story
The Only Way to Win

LEADING

WITH

CHARACTER

10 MINUTES A DAY
TO A BRILLIANT LEGACY

DR. JIM LOEHR

WITH CAREN KENNEY

WILEY

For general information on our other products and services or for technical support, please contact our Customer Care Department within the United States at (800) 762-2974, outside the United States at (317) 572-3993 or fax (317) 572-4002.

Wiley publishes in a variety of print and electronic formats and by print-on-demand. Some material included with standard print versions of this book may not be included in e-books or in print-on-demand. If this book refers to media such as a CD or DVD that is not included in the version you purchased, you may download this material at http://booksupport.wiley.com. For more information about Wiley products, visit www.wiley.com.

Library of Congress Cataloging-in-Publication Data:

Names: Loehr, Jim, author. | Kenney, Caren, author.
Title: Leading with character : 10 minutes a day to a brilliant legacy /
    Jim Loehr ; with Caren Kenney.
Description: Second Edition. | Hoboken : Wiley, 2020. | Includes index.
Identifiers: LCCN 2020029616 (print) | LCCN 2020029617 (ebook) | ISBN
    9781119550181 (hardback) | ISBN 9781119550174 (adobe pdf) | ISBN
    9781119550198 (epub)
Subjects: LCSH: Leadership. | Leadership—Moral and ethical aspects. |
    Character.
Classification: LCC HD57.7 .L6424 2020 (print) | LCC HD57.7 (ebook) | DDC
    658.4/092—dc23
LC record available at https://lccn.loc.gov/2020029616
LC ebook record available at https://lccn.loc.gov/2020029617

COVER ART AND DESIGN: PAUL MCCARTHY

Printed in the United States of America
SKY1002318_021321

To my parents, Mary and Con, and my three sons,
Michael, Patrick, and Jeffrey.

Character is destiny.
– Heraclitus

CONTENTS

FOREWORD

Leadership has never been more important than it is right now. As I write this, the world is dealing with the COVID-19 pandemic and the subsequent economic fallout. Unemployment in the United States is reaching levels not seen since the Great Depression, and economies around the globe are reporting negative GDP growth. Businesses up and down Main Street are closed, many forever. On top of this, the police killing of George Floyd in Minneapolis has fueled pent-up social and racial unrest across the country and around the world. Twenty cities in the United States are under curfew, and the military has been deployed. Trust in institutions and "the system" is falling, as uncertainty and fear grow.

Leadership in moments like this really matters. I'm talking about leaders everywhere, at all levels of society: heads of state and CEOs, leaders in our communities and in our schools, leaders in the arts, in academia, in the world of sports. Even in our own family. We all have a role to play in making the world better, and the crises we are experiencing today underscore that point.

These overlapping crises we are facing will, I believe, be the ultimate test of leadership in our lifetime. What leaders do now, and just as importantly, how they lead, will likely shape their legacy.

That means finding ways to be the leader you want to be and that our neighbors, our employees, our people, and our planet need you to be. As Jim Loehr points out in this urgent, eye-opening, and actionable book, that means leading with purpose.

Jim's is a voice that we need to hear right now, especially, as he puts it, "those of us who are fortunate enough to be in a position of leadership." His perspective on leadership – what it entails, what it requires day after day – could not be more timely.

I've been fortunate to know Jim for nearly 20 years, so I've become very familiar with the specific kind of leadership that he has been talking about over the course of his career: purpose-driven, moral, compassionate leadership born of character and nurtured by intentionality and hard work. And in this book, he gives you a clear guide to developing a personal credo that captures what you hope to accomplish through your leadership, which you then need to apply, or try to apply, at every encounter you have and every decision you make. That's how we display our true character, Jim writes, and how we "chisel our true essence from the bedrock of life, one moral decision at a time."

The book is called *Leading with Character*, and one's purpose in life is the through line, the fuel, and the catalyst for it all. In the pages that follow, you'll get what I've gotten out of my experience working with Jim over the years. It is a necessary examination of the relationship between character and leadership and what leading with character means. It is an eminently practical guide to defining one's own personal credo and to training the leadership muscles that will help you live up to it. And it is a stirring meditation on the elements of one's legacy – how it's much more about how we treat others than what we do for ourselves, and why we must work at it every single day with intent and discipline.

What you walk away with is both a framework and a toolkit for becoming a better, more thoughtful leader. It's a guide to training and strengthening your leadership muscles, much as you would train a muscle group in the gym: with focus, commitment, and determination. And it is a roadmap that, when followed with intent, will better prepare leaders to treat people as they should and to confront the challenges they will inevitably face – and that we are all facing now.

I've been in training, so to speak, and developing my "leadership muscles" for more than 40 years, while working at three "institutions." I started my career in the U.S. Army (founded 1775), which I joined out of college and where I spent four years as an officer in West Germany at the height of the Cold War. Next came Procter & Gamble (founded 1837) where I spent 28 years in Brand Management and General Management, including leading the company's business in Southeast Asia and eventually rising to Group President of the $7 billion Global Male Grooming business, when P&G made the largest acquisition ever in packaged goods, buying Gillette for $57 billion in 2005 and then running that iconic business for six years. Those experiences helped shaped me as a leader and prepared me to take on my current role, at Levi Strauss & Co. (founded 1853), where I've been the CEO for the past nine years.

The common thread between these organizations is that all three are values-led and purpose-driven, with cultures that emphasize character and a strong moral compass. That is why, I firmly believe, they have all endured for generations – through wars and economic crises, through natural disasters and pandemics, through astounding technological advancements and tumultuous social upheaval, and even through their own occasional missteps.

As a leader, I am the product of my experiences, assignments, and the leaders that I've worked for. I've also been fortunate to have wonderful mentors and coaches along the way, including, Jim Loehr.

Over the past two decades, Jim has been a coach and friend who has helped me to define who I am and the kind of leader I am today. I've worked with him on several occasions – often, I can see now, at what turned out to be critical points in my life and career. Soon after I took the helm at LS&Co., for example, he pushed me to think very intentionally about the kind of leader I wanted to be – what my legacy would be. He forced deep and occasionally uncomfortable self-reflection that involves facing brutal truths about yourself and working consistently to reach for that next level. From Jim, I learned the importance of journaling as a way to force thoughtful introspection on a daily basis. While I may miss a day or two here or there, journaling (almost) every day – and the thoughtful interrogation and self-reflection it elicits – is something that I know has contributed to my success.

It is not easy, but that's why it's so invaluable. Jim challenged me to become a purpose-driven, compassionate leader, born of character and nurtured by intentionality and hard work. And ever since, he's challenged me to keep working on it. Every day.

I joined LS&Co. for three main reasons (there are always only three reasons, right?). First, the Levi's brand. I grew up wearing Levi's, and to me it was one of the most iconic brands in the world.

Unfortunately, it had fallen into disrepair and had lost its relevance. Could it be reinvigorated? I firmly believed that it could. To me, it was a great challenge.

Second, the company's values. This was a company that commits to "Profits through Principles" and has a long legacy, going all the way back to Levi Strauss himself, of giving back and making a difference in society. We desegregated our factories in the south 10 years before it became the law of the land. We were one of the first companies to offer healthcare benefits to same-sex partners in the United States. We pulled all funding of the Boy Scouts when they banned Gay Troop Leaders in the early 1990s, and then didn't waver despite getting more than 130,000 letters and emails, almost all of which announced an intention to boycott Levi's. Making a difference and not being afraid to take a stand, even if unpopular, is what the company is made of. That resonated with me and made me want to be a part of it. And, history has proven the company's stands to be right with the benefit of hindsight.

Third, the company was in trouble. It had not created any shareholder value in over a decade. Sales had plummeted, the company was highly levered with over $2 billion of debt, and the Levi's brand had become irrelevant. My own two boys never wore Levi's as teenagers. A far cry from my generation! Back in my day, if you went to Woodstock (I was still a few years too young), you were either wearing Levi's or you were naked.

So I took the job, wanting to turn the company and the brand around, and wanting to leave a legacy, to make a difference. This was one of America's greatest brands, and one of America's oldest companies. The chance to turn the company around, make the brand what it was when I was a kid, where I begged my mom to take me two towns away to buy a pair of Levi's before I started middle school. And, I believed one key to turning the company around was to lead with our values as a company.

That is to say, I had a purpose. I had a vision of what I wanted to accomplish and what I wanted to leave behind, and that has been crucial to everything that's happened since. What's more, I gave a lot of thought to what I wanted my legacy to be: to be more about how I led rather than just the results we achieved. That we could and would get great results not just because of WHAT we did, but because of HOW we did it. Always choosing the harder right over the easier wrong. Innovating in ways that could improve the business and our industry. Not being afraid to take a stand on tough issues of our day and, in doing so, putting the Levi's brand back at the center of culture.

Over the past seven years, we've delivered revenue and profit growth every single year, excluding the impacts of foreign exchange, and we've created significant shareholder value. The Levi's brand has arguably never been stronger. Sales last year were $5.9 billion, up from $4.6 billion when I joined. We successfully returned the company to the public markets in March 2019 with a very successful IPO, and at that time I recommitted that we were not backing off of our values even as a public company.

As much success as we've had as a company over the last seven years I am more proud of HOW we did it. What made us successful through the turnaround was our commitment to those values. Never have I been more convinced about the importance of leading with character. We doubled down on our values. We have innovated around sustainability and have not backed away from the Paris Climate Agreement and our commitment to reduce our carbon footprint. We are innovating with lasers and with new fibers, like cottonized hemp, both of which require dramatically less water than their legacy counterparts. In 2016, when the president banned immigration from seven Muslim countries, we were very quick to take a stand on this unprecedented unilateral Executive action. Not only did we speak out against it publicly, we also supported court cases with amicus briefs. And, importantly, we put our money where our mouth was and committed dollars from the Levi Strauss Foundation to support non-profit organizations around the country to support marginalized communities impacted by the Executive Order.

In 2018 after the Parkland shooting in Florida, we decided to take a stand to end gun violence in America. Every day, 100 people in this country die as a result of tragic gun violence. Every death is a sad one. Almost everyone knows someone who has died as a result of gun violence. Our children today practice lockdown drills at school, just like we practiced "duck and cover" drills to protect us from nuclear bombs from the Soviet Union when I was a kid. However, unlike the nuclear bombs from the Soviet Union, which never happened, our kids know that school shootings are a real threat – they see it on the news and they know that it happens. Their lives have been forever impacted by school shootings and lockdown drills. It is one of the most contentious issues of our day – but staying silent on the issue longer was not an option for us.

Our goal is not to repeal the Second Amendment. It is to end senseless, needless gun violence, which is possible. In January of 2019, we wrote a letter to the House of Representatives to support HR 8, which called for universal background checks, a proven measure that a majority of gun owners support, to reduce guns getting into the wrong hands. The legislation passed with bipartisan support. The letter to the House had three CEO signatures on it, besides mine. Later, in September 2019, we sent a similar letter to the Senate, to get the Senate to move on its counterpart bill. That letter had over 160 CEO signatures. By being the point of the spear along with three other CEOs in January, we have built a movement of business leaders to make a difference in ending tragic gun violence in this country. We are not done with our work – but election season is upon us, and we are not giving up.

I will end where I started. The COVID pandemic has wiped out much of the financial progress we've made as a company. As proud as I am of the turnaround, I now know that my legacy as a CEO will be around HOW we navigate the pandemic and residual crises around it. Our 3100 retail stores around the world and most of our wholesale customers' stores have been closed for over two months. Our revenues, like many retailers, have taken a hit, and I suspect the recovery, and our return to $6 billion in sales, will take time. We are navigating the most uncertain time I've ever faced in my career. People have been working from home for nearly three months now. Uncertainty and volatility are our daily challenges.

But through it all, I continue to be guided to make the hard decisions in the grey area by following our values and committing to "do the harder right over the easier wrong" at every step. It's not easy, balancing all of the critical stakeholders in the business: shareholders (including family members – descendants of Levi Strauss), employees, retirees, partners, suppliers, and customers. It is a fragile ecosystem with massive uncertainty, and weighing it all requires a strong moral compass and a conviction, above all else, to do what is right.

I can draw a direct line from much of this to the time I've spent with Jim and the lessons and exercises he discusses in the pages that follow. They have been a fantastic resource for me over my career, and I know they can benefit you, too. *Leading with Character* can help you sharpen and define your potential legacy and in the course of doing that, will make you a better leader in all aspects of your life.

Chip Bergh,
President and CEO of Levi Strauss & Co

PREFACE

Eleven years ago, I was incredibly fortunate to be a student of Dr. Jim Loehr's, as I attended training he led at the Human Performance Institute (HPI), which he co-founded with Dr. Jack Groppel 25 years ago. The experience at HPI in Orlando, Florida, was life changing. Jim guided me through the difficult and important work of facing the truth about how I was managing my energy, and who and what was getting the best of it; and he pushed me to engage in soul-searching to define my purpose and life mission. I had to rewrite "my story," identify strategies to become more physically energized and mentally and emotionally resilient, and lay out a plan to ensure that when I depart this Earth, I will leave a legacy I can be proud of, measured by my impact on the people who mean the most to me.

Since then, I have been blessed to call Jim a dear friend, mentor, and colleague who continues to profoundly impact my life. His work was foundational to the Premier Executive Leadership™ program, which I was honored to have the opportunity to build for the Human Performance Institute in 2016 and continue to lead. This first-of-a-kind executive development and well-being program takes a whole-person, whole-life approach to helping leaders thrive in an increasingly complex, nonstop, stressful world. It leverages an integrated three-coach approach (executive coach, exercise physiologist, and registered dietitian), 360 stakeholder interviews, family engagement and training to create an ecosystem of support, a comprehensive executive health assessment, and assessments in energy, well-being, resilience, and character strength. The assessment and training on building character strength is one of the unique components of this program. While other leadership training has focused on leadership authenticity (which is different from character) and the media are beginning to focus on the character of the company, few if any focus on the leader's personal character, which is the content of one's legacy. It is a "muscle" that can be strengthened and is arguably the most important component of this training.

I am incredibly honored to have the opportunity to contribute to this book and share what we learned through our work with some of the many global leaders who have passed through the Institute; through intimate engagements with our Premier clients that provide a rare view of the complex and personal struggles leaders face today; through my one-on-one coaching and engagement with executive clients; and our ongoing research into how best to unleash potential for leaders and others who want to become the best possible versions of themselves, in the most meaningful areas of their lives.

And there has never been a more important time to focus on character – not only because leadership dismissals due to ethical lapses are at an all-time high, but because the complexity and stakes are now larger than ever due to the increasing demands, scrutiny, and expectations placed on leaders today. The current COVID-19 pandemic provides a perfect example of the intense moral dilemma faced by business, government, and healthcare leaders throughout the world. But this goes beyond being a business, political, or healthcare issue. It's a moral issue, deeply connected to our families, our jobs, our welfare – with life or death consequences. Leaders have to choose between stakeholder health and well-being and shareholder financial rights . . . between abiding by mandatory government shut-down of all non-essential businesses to prevent the spread of the virus and honoring civil liberties guaranteed by the Bill of Rights . . . between saving lives by the enforced closing of businesses and the loss of jobs that force some into bankruptcy and poverty . . . between who gets prioritized medical attention and access to a life-saving ventilator that is in short supply . . . and who is left to die. The pandemic descended upon us like a tidal wave with no preparation or playbook. The fast-moving, unpredictable, and deadly virus required swift daily decision-making despite multiple unknowns, no easy answers, and the fact that any and every decision would have painful consequences. While many of us are fortunate to not have been in the position to make some of the heart-wrenching decisions related to the pandemic, we will continually be called upon to make difficult choices in our lives that have an impact on others and the world around us – often in a very profound way. The good news is that we now have the opportunity to develop our own playbook and moral compass so that we are prepared for the inevitable storms and dilemmas that will test, tempt, and challenge us – and lead with character, confidence, and a strong connection to our deepest values. But we must first do the work.

To live a successful life and achieve a meaningful leadership legacy require a deep connection to a purpose focused outside oneself and intentional, ongoing investment in the strengthening of one's character. This book will expose the character vulnerability that lies below the surface in each of us and take you through training exercises designed to strengthen your Character Muscle – or collection of muscles, really – so that vulnerability is vanquished. It will guide you through the most important moments and decisions in your life, critical episodes we may be ill-equipped to manage if we haven't done the character work necessary to meet those moments. Grandiose as it may sound, this book can help you to achieve a personal legacy that will transcend your time on this Earth.

Caren Kenney

Only one kind of leadership can successfully respond to a moral crisis: moral leadership. It's especially in times of crisis that people naturally look to authority for truthful answers, wise guidance, courageous action, and hope.

– Dov Seidman, author of *How*

Introduction

Somehow, against all odds, you were born. You were granted the gift of life. The actual probability of your being born is beyond comprehension. Regardless of the jaw-dropping unlikelihood, you made the cut and won the lottery we call life. You are here.

So why you? You had no hand in making it happen. Through no effort of yours, you simply appeared. What have you done with this gift?

Three facts are immutable: You were born. You will die. And between your birth and death is the opportunity for impact.

What is your impact so far? What has happened, for better or worse, because you are here? Have you represented yourself well? Have you proven worthy of the sacred gift?

To help answer such questions, fast-forward to just beyond the end of your life. Even though you have passed away, let's imagine you get to witness a very special happening: your own memorial service. But this service is different in a couple of ways (aside from the most obvious – that you're able to witness it): For one, *all* of your loved ones and meaningful connections are there, even those who pre-deceased you – family members including parents and grandparents; friends from childhood through old age; coworkers and those above and below you from all your professional endeavors; mentors and mentees; classmates, neighbors, teammates, military brothers and sisters, fellow congregants, local merchants – in short, anyone whose life was touched by yours. And this service is unlike most in another way: Everyone there has been summoned to tell their *absolute truth* about you. That's not to say that people at non-imaginary funerals *don't* tell the truth . . . but let's face it: Some of them don't. They tend to gloss over the not-so-good stuff. And people who might not have glowing things to say about the deceased are often not in attendance.

In the case of this special service that you get to witness, even those who were not so fond of you will be in attendance and invited to speak. Everyone is gathered there to express, with complete frankness, what impact your life had on theirs: what happened to them *because of you*.

As the attendees reflect, one by one, it becomes clear to you that, despite the fact you are no longer physically present, you endure in their lives in a quite tangible way.

This is your legacy.

Legacy is the trace you leave. Every life leaves a trace, a trace that may exist for generations. Your legacy is the sum total of the impact your life made on the lives of others – and, in many ways, the trace that *their* life makes on others.

To best comprehend your impact, you listen very carefully to what each person at your funeral says about you. (After all, you're dead, so it's not as if you have something else to do.)

You listen as your mother and father describe what happened to each of them because of you. What was the net effect of your life on theirs?

Next to speak is your partner, spouse, or significant other. What was your impact on and contribution to that relationship? Did he or she feel truly loved and valued? Did he or she get your best energy when you came home at the end of the day, and your full attention when you were together?

If you have children, what is each son or daughter saying as they describe how your influence exists in them, for better or worse? What are they saying about how your life impacted who they are now and what they have become? Are they expressing the belief they are better human beings because of you? What part of your legacy's impact on them are you *not* proud of? Makes you wince? Makes you sad? Makes you smile or tear up with joy or burst with pride?

Next up: your friends. What do they begin with? Were you always there for them? Did you show compassion for them, and step up and lend a hand when life turned against them? Did you do that all the time or only some of the time? Did you do it only when it was convenient for you or always when it mattered to them? Were you loyal? As they talk, what are the traits that they share that seem to repeat, from one friend to the next to the next? Are the memories they share the ones you would have guessed?

Last to speak are all those associated with your life at work. It's a big lineup. Bosses, clients, direct reports, co-workers, assistants, support staff, and so on. Even valets, janitors, and security will be asked to remember. Each one will describe your impact on them individually, how you treated them in good times and bad, even when you were stressed, tired, or unhappy. Listen as they speak about your respectfulness, your kindness, your generosity. What does each have to say about your integrity, your honesty, your trustworthiness? How often do they comment on your humility, your moral courage, your empathy?

It's interesting, isn't it, that as all these people describe your legacy, not a single one, from any part of your life, spends significant time referencing your intelligence, titles, competence, wealth, power, achievements, academic credentials, or celebrity. From all they say, it's clear that what mattered most was simply your treatment of them, and your treatment of those who mattered to them. For each person whose life you touched, your legacy was not about your money but your kindness; not about your prominence or even fame but your integrity; not about your intelligence but your caring and respect.

That simple, undeniable, profound truth is the purpose of this book. *Leading with Character* establishes the true meaning of legacy, connecting it directly to your ethical and moral character. Ethics typically refers to a set or code of guidelines that define accepted practices and behavior for a certain group. Morality refers to the judgment as to whether an action is right or wrong. The two words will be used interchangeably throughout the book. *Leading with Character* provides a practical, daily pathway for you to build character – and, just as important in our complicated and harsh world, it provides protection against regular and formidable onslaughts.

After reflecting on all the feedback you may have received from individuals in every dimension of your life, how do you rate yourself on your character/legacy scorecard? This book was written to help current and future leaders excel on this scorecard, the scale of measurement that matters most in life.

Based on the decades I have spent studying character and legacy, and nearly 30 years coaching and training global leaders at the Institute, here are some truths we have learned:

- The morality system shared by leaders – virtually *all* leaders – is deeply flawed, placing their legacy at serious risk.

- Most leaders have very little idea just how much the moral grounding of their judgments and decision-making is often contaminated, hijacked, or corrupted (often all three).

- The sum total of the countless moral decisions a leader makes every day – trying to do and say the right thing – defines his or her legacy and that of the company or organization that he or she represents.

- A leader's ability to make sound moral and ethical judgments and follow through on them, time and again, forms his or her character. Corporate governance should (but often does not) value this ability at the highest level.

- Character is not static but a muscle that can – and should – be continually strengthened and reinforced. Leaders who recognize this dynamic make the investment of time and energy, thereby creating the path to a meaningful legacy, one that transcends their careers and lives.

The purpose of this book is threefold:

1. To expose the ingenious ways that leaders knowingly and unknowingly cross moral and ethical lines to get their personal wants and needs met.

2. To prevent leaders from defaulting to reflexive, automatic decisions of a moral nature by raising awareness about the

conscious or unconscious processes they are likely using to render these decisions.

3. To provide leaders with a proven method for building a strong and meaningful life and leadership legacy by constructing a robust Personal Credo. This will become their source code for vetting all their future ethical decisions, thereby protecting and bolstering their own legacy and that of the organizations they lead.

Issues of morality and ethical character are profoundly complex. Look no further than the intersection of morality and politics. Take a moment to ponder each of the following words or phrases.

Abortion	Gateway drug	Pacifism
Activist judges	Gun control	Patriotism
Capital punishment	Immigration	Right to life
Climate change	Legalization of drugs	Right to protest
Conservatism	Liberalism	Sanctuary cities
Duty	Mass incarceration	Terrorism
Exceptionalism	Multiculturalism	The American flag
Fossil fuels	Open borders	

Do any of these words or phrases produce a strong, visceral reaction in you? To what extent are these political/cultural issues indistinguishable from moral issues? As a quick exercise, pick the three phrases from the list above where your gut reaction was strongest. Now reflect on these questions:

- Can you pinpoint the origin of your intense emotional response?

- How convinced are you that your gut response is right? Have you ever considered that your gut might be wrong?

- Are your reactions based on facts or feelings? Do you consider what your gut tells you to be a personal belief or a verifiable truth? If you consider it to be a verifiable truth, how knowledgeable are you of all the facts on both sides of the issue?

- What's the chance that your gut response could ever be reversed? How about when you're confronted with contradictory evidence?

- Do you uniformly respect the intellect, experience, and character of those on the same side of these issues as you, and who believe as strongly as you do?

- Do you know people who feel just as strongly as you do about such issues but in the exact opposite direction? What makes you sure that your judgment is right and theirs wrong? Do you respect their intellect, experience, and character, though you strongly disagree with them?

Questions like these point to one of the flaws in our moral operating system. When our beliefs are false yet loaded with powerful emotion (as they so often are), they masquerade as fact-based truth. Given the fundamental unsoundness of our beliefs, our moral reasoning and decision-making can become tragically derailed. Political issues, which often trigger red-hot emotions, serve as vivid examples of this operational flaw. The combination of personal beliefs, ideology, and strong emotion can completely overwhelm our capacity for rational thought and sound judgment. Once we declare a belief to be unfettered truth, we close the door to introspective inquiry. Rather than using our powers of reason to investigate weaknesses and inconsistencies in what could well be a faulty belief, we instead use our capacity for creative logic to garner support for what our gut tells us to believe. Once a belief is successfully dressed up as truth (e.g., to succeed in business, it's necessary to cross moral lines; kindness and compassion in the business world are signs of weakness; most people cannot be trusted; accomplishing the mission is more important than how we accomplish it; etc.), we feel justified in whatever moral judgment or decision we render. When we detect no problem in our moral machinery, we see no reason to expend energy to rebuild it. Instead, we march forward, trusting that the coordinates in our moral GPS have all been punched in correctly; and if that's so, then how can we possibly *not* lead lives of integrity, honesty, trustworthiness, and courage? And when the system fails, and we as leaders find ourselves having breached previously sacred moral boundaries (often repeatedly), we are shocked and mortified. "How did I get here? How could I let myself do this? This is so not like me!"

From the work we have done with extraordinary colleagues and clients at the Johnson & Johnson Human Performance Institute (HPI[1]), we came to understand that "leading with character" is *not* an instinct; it is *not* a natural human response. You needn't have read Darwin to know that it is natural and instinctual to put ourselves first, to get *our* needs and wants met before those of others. Me first: That's precisely what the morality system we all inherited is programmed to consider. Becoming a leader where morality – in short, our treatment of others – is afforded the highest priority demands a *trained* response, one that requires dedicated energy investment throughout our lives.

For more than a decade at the Institute, we have searched for a practical method to build and maintain a robust personal morality system for leaders to address the inherent flaws in their morality operating system.

We believe we have found that method. This book, along with the accompanying journal, provides the map.

Most leaders go their entire professional lives without an intentionally crafted, deliberately constructed Personal Credo. (Indeed, far too many leaders don't even realize that something very big and important is missing from their lives). To answer this need, and to address other issues critical to any leader at the dawn of the third decade of the first century of the second millennium, we have included a highly scripted, easy-to-follow program of daily journaling – 10 minutes a day, for three months. Current and future leaders who are brave and committed enough to follow this program, who are intent on creating

---

[1] The Human Performance Institute (HPI) was founded by Dr. Jim Loehr and Dr. Jack Groppel in 1992. The company was sold to Johnson & Johnson in 2008. Over 250,000 people across the globe – including top global C-suite executives – have participated in programs offered by the Institute.

a brilliant legacy for themselves and their organizations, will find that it raises moral awareness – specifically, how moral decisions are made and how self-serving motivations too often drive them. It also provides a concrete method for building one's own Personal Credo, as well as specific strategies for strengthening 50 character competencies that form the basis of strong character and, hence, a brilliant legacy.

The potential value in daily, self-reflective writing cannot be overstated. In all our years working with people on such exercises, *no one* – not one person – has come away saying she or he was unchanged for the better; for most people, the experience is life-changing. Building the habit of thoughtful, goal-oriented journal writing brings extraordinary value and produces a trove of life-altering insights. And the benefits begin accruing almost immediately.

A warning: This focus on character and legacy is not for the faint-hearted. It may be one of the most difficult challenges you will ever embrace. If you're concerned, my response to you is exactly what it has been to the thousands of leaders we have worked with:

Stay the course!

You will not regret it.

CHAPTER 1

What Does "Leading with Character" Mean?

You cannot dream yourself into a character; you must hammer and forge yourself one. —Henry David Thoreau

The challenges we confront every day to remain true to our deepest values and finest character are common to all of us who are fortunate enough to be in positions of leadership. We desire to rise above our parochial self-interest and become leaders whose moral character is beyond reproach. The effort to do so is a mighty struggle.

MY FIRST EXPOSURE TO EVIL

I came face-to-face with evil at the impressionable age of 16. It was my second summer working for a cemetery and crematorium, a job that would help me earn the $200 I needed to buy my first car, a used 1949 Ford Coupe with well over 100,000 miles. My first summer of cemetery work was tough but manageable: I watered the grass for large plots filled with every conceivable type of gravestone – small to large, simple to ornate, cheap to very expensive. The cemetery was lush, with endless lines of old trees that often provided inviting cool shade for me as I worked. I came to know every inch of the lots I maintained. Reading the inscriptions on the gravestones helped fill the time. The size and ornamental detail of the monument were always far less moving to me than the words etched on them: *kind . . . loving . . . faithful . . . integrity*. Even at 16, I couldn't help but wonder what words I would like inscribed on my grave, to represent who I had been while I was

9

here. Though I made all of 90 cents an hour, I found working in and among graves to be strangely rewarding – until the following summer.

At the start of my second stint, my boss approached me with an offer I couldn't refuse – an opportunity to earn a 20-cent hourly boost. $1.10 per hour! It was a dream come true. With the extra money, I could definitely buy my car by summer's end, maybe even before.

"Do you have the stomach for hard work, son?" my boss asked.

"Absolutely!" I responded without hesitation, though I wondered if he thought what I had done the previous summer didn't qualify as hard work. "What would I be doing?"

It was labor of a different order – far different. I would complete a four-man grave-digging repair crew. "When graves start sinking in," explained my boss, "it can mean that the top of the casket collapsed. So it's got to be repaired and sealed. Your crew removes the grass and dirt so the grave can be examined and the necessary repairs can be made. If the top cracks and collapses, we bring in a rig to lift a new top into place." He paused, then smiled, as if preparing me for the real message. "If there's considerable damage, you may find yourself looking directly into caskets. You'll see decaying bodies. Are you okay with that?"

The only thing on my mind was the $1.10 per hour, and just which week in August – maybe even July! – I would finally have enough to purchase my Ford Coupe.

"I think so," I said, unperturbed by his cautioning words.

The boss took me to meet my crew. To this day, they remain perhaps the three scariest human beings I have ever met.

The crew chief was named Kentucky. His face terrified me. His piercing eyes burned right through me – so withering and frightening that I had to look away: I simply could not look at him directly. I'm sure I appeared to him as if I had seen a ghost. When my boss left, Kentucky grabbed me by the T-shirt sleeve and yanked me away from the other two men.

"Who the f— are you!?" he demanded in a broken, raspy voice. It was not a question I believed I could answer.

I said nothing; I *couldn't*. It felt as if my breathing had shut down. Kentucky jerked me close, inches from his face. "Look at me, boy! Let me tell you who I am. I've killed eleven people in my life, so far. I've buried them all so no one will ever find them. If you *ever* speak about what you're going to see, you'll be number 12. Got it?!"

I still couldn't manage a sound.

"*Got it?!*" he screamed in my face.

I nodded.

After we cleared the first gravesite, the three men jumped in and began looting everything of value: rings, jewelry, even a belt buckle. The corpse was floating in water that had seeped in through the damaged casket. I was in a state of near-shock, beyond horrified. The three grave robbers picked the casket and corpse clean of any remnant of monetary value. They hopped up and out, and once again Kentucky yanked me right up to his face. "One word and you're number 12!" he hissed.

We broke for lunch, and I excused myself. I found my boss and told him the work was too hard for me. I wanted my old job back, and would happily take the pay cut.

I had nightmares for months. I didn't tell my parents what happened because I was sure that Kentucky would somehow find out.

The moment I witnessed those three ghoulish characters robbing that grave, I understood that evil existed in the world. My eyes had been opened. I also felt ashamed because, at least in this virgin test case, I did nothing to stop it, and knew I never would take any steps to stop it. I was too afraid. Throughout the summer, a day did not go by that I didn't count in my head how many graves I imagined they were robbing that I might have prevented, had I possessed the courage to report it.

Thus began my lifelong quest to explore the world of character.

I don't know, of course, if you've ever come face to face with evil as I did, or whether you will ever look back on an episode in your life and deeply regret, as I still do, what you did – or didn't do – about it.

From other incidents in my life, I realized that the evil I witnessed at the cemetery that summer was not a one-time thing. I learned, sadly, that evil was not as much an outlier as I had once thought. Fortunately, I can also say, even more forcefully, that despite the deeply troubling behaviors I have witnessed, they are dwarfed in number by the many, many acts of goodness, selflessness, and even heroism that I have witnessed. It is this behavior that stands out for me as the more enduring, salient expression of human nature.

Yes, the forces of corruption, greed, hypocrisy, immorality, and evil are real and formidable. They are unavoidable. If one is not careful, these forces can beat you down, corrupt you, seduce you, damage you, depress you; they can *change* you. Yet there are so many pivotal moments in life where the decision you make determines which forces triumph: immorality, meanness, unfairness, criminality – lack of character; or morality, kind-heartedness, generosity, justice – noble character.

With just a few concentrated minutes of soulful reflection a day, something nearly miraculous happens: You actually *build* your ethical and moral character.

Every leader is morally broken in some way. Some are in pieces. We all can get better.

THE MEANING OF CHARACTER

The word "character" comes from the Greek word, "kharakter," a chisel or marking instrument for stone or metal. In a sense, we chisel our true essence from the bedrock of life, one moral decision at a time. Character is who we really were when we were here.

Our unique mark exists both within us and within those we lead. Our mark, chiseled throughout our lifetime, becomes our legacy, and plays a powerful role in the legacy of all those who follow us. To be a leader means to influence from the front, with intention. As leaders, we are culture creators; leading with character means to create, consciously and intentionally, a culture where ethics and morality are celebrated, and given the highest priority. Every word, every gesture, every decision forms a mark, however big or small, on our character, as well as on the culture we create around us.

The financial crisis of 2007–2008 is a powerful example of what can happen when leaders fail to lead with character. The pain and suffering caused by the staggering loss of trillions of dollars in some ways can be reduced to mere numbers, and in other ways is incalculable. In the United States alone, 1.2 million jobs were lost in 2008, another 1.3 million in 2009. People lost homes and life savings, were forced into bankruptcy, lost the ability to pay for their children's college education, lost hope for retirement. How did the most destructive financial crisis since the Great Depression happen, a crisis that decimated the hopes, dreams, and futures of millions? How were the massive failures of corporate governance and risk management allowed to occur? Why did regulators fail to disclose conflicts of interest? How did credit-rating agencies fail to rein in Wall Street's excesses? How and why did overvaluation of bundled subprime mortgages happen? What was the rationale for easy credit, a lack of transparency, dubious (and downright fraudulent) underwriting practices, predatory lending, and incentivizing loan officers to entice borrowers to take out unsecured loans? How was it that conflicts of interest between professional investment managers and institutional clients were never called out? Why did deregulation of over-the-counter derivatives, especially credit default swaps, go unchecked? How did relaxed underwriting standards by Fannie Mae and Freddie Mac take place without tighter scrutiny? Why did Lehman Brothers get swept into bankruptcy, and Bear Stearns and Merrill Lynch get sold at fire-sale prices? What precipitated Goldman Sachs and Morgan Stanley, in the brutal aftermath, becoming commercial banks, subject to tighter regulation and controls?

The answers to all these questions bring us to a core thesis of this book: Leaders actually *have* incredible power to prevent catastrophes like the financial meltdown of 2007–2008 from occurring in the first place. Whether they exercise that power, individually or collectively, is of course a very different matter. How many bank officials, Wall Street traders, financial advisors, institutional investors, government officials, banking regulators, financial media cheerleaders, and on and on (and on), knew in their hearts that something about what was going on, or what they were doing, wasn't right? How many of these people recognized that ethical lines were being crossed but simply chose to do nothing about it? (Because, of course, doing nothing is a choice.) How many of these people realized that the financial gravy train that was speeding down the tracks was going to crash – who knew, from the numbers, that it simply couldn't last – but whose first priority was to cash in before everything blew up? Could that worldwide crisis and all the pain and suffering endured by so many be traced back to simple greed, which occasioned a failure on the part of leaders to uphold moral standards in return for their personal or their organization's financial gain? What might have happened if more leaders had stepped forward and led, first and foremost, with character?

I'm certain there were leaders who *did* step up, who refused to become complicit in what they believed to be unethical practices. Unfortunately, their voices were too few and too muted to stop the financial train wreck. I wonder how many executives lost their jobs, were denied promotions, bonuses, and salary increases because they were not onboard with what was happening. What were the consequences for dragging their feet and asking tough ethical questions? Who were those people who raised red flags and suffered serious consequences for questioning the system? Aren't these outliers unsung heroes whose ethical spine will never be recognized or celebrated?

I know. That's a lot of questions. The most important ones of all are these: Why did those who stepped up do so, and how were they able to? What enabled some men and women to transcend the coercive, seductive, go-along-to-get-along power of a culture of greed, to challenge their superiors and perhaps colleagues and take the contrary moral stand? And why did those who didn't speak up – the many, many who didn't – do what they did instead?

By the end of this book, you should have the answers.

A VIEW FROM THE TOP OF THE MOUNTAIN

I was born and raised in Colorado and developed a deep love for the Rocky Mountains and all that they had to offer, particularly climbing its numerous majestic peaks. There are 58 peaks of 14,000 feet or more. I will never forget the view from atop the "fourteeners" that I was fortunate enough to climb. On the ascent, my focus was typically just a few feet in front of me. Occasionally I would stop and look over the terrain below, but that vantage was quite limited compared to the panoramic view I would eventually enjoy. A whole new perspective suddenly appeared at the summit. My view of reality was expanded and broadened instantly.

A similar shift in perspective has occurred to me regarding the roles that character and legacy play in a person's life. The difference has been much slower to evolve than the dramatic disparity I noticed within a few hours on a mountain climb, but the clarity I now possess in advanced age is as bracing as that view from the top of a fourteener on a clear day.

The strength of our Character Muscles is best revealed when they are put under pressure.

I only wish I could have had this perspective much earlier in life. I would have done several things quite differently. Perspective changes everything because perspective is our reality. When I reflect on my life, my parents, my three sons, the business leaders I have come to know, the hundreds of athletes I have been privileged to work with (including 17 world #1s in their respective sports or competitions); when I reflect on my friends, partners, business associates, employees, and personal mentors, the issue of moral strength towers over all other considerations. Because of my age, the panoramic view I now have spans five generations – my grandparents, my parents, my children, my seven grandchildren.

Confirming the truth about the moral character of any individual is difficult, even for those who have known that person for years, even when that person is a family member. How many times have you been shocked to learn that someone you thought you knew well had suffered a tragic moral collapse? Weaknesses in our muscles of integrity, honesty, trustworthiness, and so on can be hidden from view for years, until one day the deficiency is finally exposed. Why does it surface when it does? Usually it's brought on by a highly stressful event. As it is with physical strength, the strength of our character muscles is most accurately revealed when they are put under pressure. In such high-stress moments, you can't pretend or lie that you are stronger than you are; in those moments, you are who you are.

Stress comes in many forms, of course. In the case I mean here – stress-testing our character strength – that pressure is very often the lure of wealth, the pain of bankruptcy, or the perceived embarrassment and disgrace of divorce (to name three common examples). Stress builds to often unbearable levels when we find ourselves consumed by strong emotions like envy, jealously, greed, anger, fear, or resentment. Extreme stress may come about because of a protracted health crisis, the threat of being demoted if you don't get onboard with the agenda, an office romance (or even the prospect or "threat" of one). All of these instances are stressful and can place extraordinary demands on our moral muscles. The moral stress demands generated by the 2007–2008 financial crisis clearly exceeded the limits of thousands of men and women working in the financial industry. These people had, for the most part, solid employment histories, and reputations for trustworthiness, honesty, and generally high integrity. They were good mothers and fathers, good sons and daughters, good spouses and partners, community-minded citizens. But the demands of the financial crisis exceeded their ethical limits. And rather than taking action and raising a red flag, they instead looked the other way. Equally disturbing, they assumed little or no responsibility for the carnage that followed. From their perspective, they were simply doing what everyone else was doing. They were doing what they were told. They were being good soldiers. Because their character muscles were not built to withstand the stress of the moment, they were simply incapable of leading with character.

Adversity does not build character, it reveals it. —James Lane Allen

---

TRAINING THE CHARACTER MUSCLES OF LEADERS

Most corporate leaders acknowledge that sustained business success is threatened when leaders cross ethical lines to accomplish their objectives. Many of the greatest collapses in business history occurred in the wake of such lapses – Enron, WorldCom, Arthur Andersen, Bernie Madoff, The Weinstein Company, and countless others. BP, Wells Fargo, and Volkswagen have seen their reputations profoundly damaged because of unethical behavior by their leaders. More recently, WeWork and Theranos saw their perceived values collapse because of highly dubious behavior on the part of Adam Neumann and Elizabeth Holmes, their respective leaders. (One may reasonably argue that, in both cases, their perceived value was never close to their intrinsic value.) According to the June 2017 issue of *Harvard Business Review*, the five-year period from 2012 to 2016 saw a 36% increase in the number of CEOs dismissed for ethical lapses, compared to 2007–2011. This conduct included fraud, bribery, sexual indiscretion, insider trading, and more. In 2018, CEO dismissals for ethical lapses exceeded dismissals for financial performance or board struggles for the first time in history.

Today, CEO turnover is at an all-time high. According to *HBR*, 50–60% of executives fail within the first 18 months of being promoted or hired, and there's a rise in leadership failure due to issues such as stress, burnout, and unethical decisions and behavior. A Harvard Medical School study found that 96% of senior leaders reported feeling burned out, with one-third describing the burnout as "extreme."

It will come as no surprise to you that burnout – especially extreme burnout – often negatively affects decision-making.

Of course, this character crisis is not just a corporate leadership problem – it's a problem of leadership across industries and once-hallowed institutions. Although it's natural to exaggerate the problems in one's own era and lose sight of where one stands historically, I think it's fair to say that these are not inspiring times for leadership (to take a few, but certainly not all, examples) in the Catholic Church, the U.S. Congress, Wall Street, many professional and high-level college sports leagues and teams, education, media, health care, global diplomacy, and on and on. And on.

Nor is character deficiency just a leadership problem: It's a culture-wide problem. We have fewer good, actual human examples to inspire us. So many of us have numbed ourselves to accepting poor character in our leaders – and in ourselves! – if and when it serves our needs and wants.

You're offended at a TV show with lots of foul language and immoral behavior . . . yet somehow you support and vote for political leaders who engage in both, frequently.

You believe that certain military actions are immoral when taken by "the other side" (say, drone use) . . . but when it's your side that's doing it, it's justifiable.

You deplore any sort of cheating, and teach your children that it's wrong . . . yet when it's your beloved hometown team that's accused (see Spygate, Deflategate, baseball's sign-stealing scandal, dubious college recruiting practices, looking the other way on reprehensible behavior by star athletes, etc.), you go to work rationalizing or downplaying the bad behavior.

If our leaders are not generally of high character, then it's a real problem for all of us.

As most C-suite executives will readily admit, it's one thing to recognize the threat of character deficiency – and quite another to provide a viable solution to diminish or eliminate the threat. As one CEO told me, "We've tried several things. None has been successful. The character of leaders is tricky territory. It's easy to sound preachy, moralistic, to cross sensitive religious boundaries." He went on to describe how his company's efforts in compliance training and ethics classes had fallen far short of expectations. "There appears to be built-in resistance to training character because it becomes deeply personal, *fast*. For some people, just being *asked* to take a character training course feels like an indictment of their character."

Despite these and many other barriers, we at the Human Performance Institute were determined to find an answer to the question: How can leaders lead with character? To answer that, though, we first had to answer this question: How can character be developed and strengthened?

The stakes for these questions and answers could not be higher.

And after more than 10 years of research and concentrated trial and error work at HPI, we found the answers.

Our approach, called Leading with Character, begins with two fundamental ideas.

First: One's character is best understood as specific competencies that can be trained (as referenced earlier) in the same way that muscles of the physical body are trained. Character strengths, such as integrity, trustworthiness, compassion, justice, and so forth, are developed much the way that bicep or quadricep strength is acquired: through energy investment. Converting weak muscles of character into strengths requires strategic energy investment in the muscles targeted for growth. Detailing that process represents an important component of this training system.

The second fundamental idea: Character is best thought of as existing in two distinct but related categories of competency – **performance** character competency and **moral** character competency. Performance character consists of specific acquired strengths usually necessary for high achievement and performance: focus, persistence, resilience, confidence, positivity, decisiveness, courage, tough-mindedness, ambition, reliability, discipline, fortitude.

Take a moment to reflect on the relative priority each of the above traits has in your life. Which three have the highest priority? Competencies such as these reflect the personal assets one must acquire to fulfill his or her highest *performance* potential, to achieve at the highest level.

It's imperative to understand that the muscles of performance character *are not linked in any way* to principles of right or wrong; there is no connection between them and morality. Performance character strengths support high achievement whether the achiever crosses moral lines or not.

Kenneth Lay, Martha Stewart, Ivan Boesky, Michael Milken, John Riggs, Dennis Kozlowski, Jeffrey Skilling, Bernard Ebbers, Bernie Madoff, Barry Bonds, Harvey Weinstein, Les Moonves, and Alex Cora all possessed an impressive portfolio of performance character strengths. None of their performance character muscles, however, protected them from serious lapses in moral judgment or ethical behavior.

The second dimension of character – ethical/moral character – consists of highly specific acquired competencies (muscles) that support ethical behavior and enhance moral judgment and reasoning. Moral character reflects the values we hold in the treatment of others.

Bernie Ebbers, CEO of World Com; Kenneth Lay, chairman of Enron; and Dennis Kozlowski, CEO of Tyco, were identified as among the 50 best most successful leaders in America, and not long after, all three were indicted for white-collar crime and sent to prison.

The following list is representative: moral integrity,[1] love, honesty, kindness, trustworthiness, humility, compassion, gratitude, generosity, moral courage, empathy, loyalty.

---

[1] At the ends of chapters you will find several Character Call-Outs, each of which amplifies on a character strength, performance, or moral. The character strength is defined and followed by suggestions for strengthening it in yourself, in those you lead at work, and with family members at home. Differences between some character strengths are very subtle – e.g., personal courage and moral courage, kindness and affection, compassion and empathy. As in the physical body, these capacities represent supportive muscles that are closely linked and functionally related.

Again, take a moment to reflect on the relative priority of each of these traits in your life. Which three have the highest priority for you?

Performance character drives *what* we achieve.

Moral character drives *how* we achieve it.

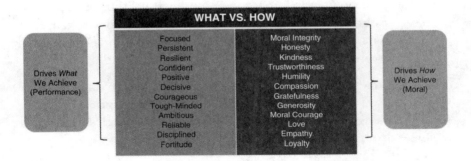

A tenet of this book is that leading with ethical character is the more important dimension of organizational leadership for creating and sustaining a brilliant legacy.[2]

LET'S DO SOME INTROSPECTION

Some questions to ponder:

When was the last time your ethical strength was seriously tested? What made the situation so difficult for you? Did you pass or fail the test?

Perhaps you falsified information on your professional résumé. Or you fired someone who didn't deserve it. Was your failure in the judgment itself or in not following through on the judgment? To what extent did fatigue, lack of sleep, poor nutrition, and so forth contribute to your character failure?

Let's do some more introspection. Have you ever driven your car knowing your blood alcohol level was likely above the legal limit? Did you consider the risks to others? Have you ever accelerated your car to dangerous speeds, run red lights, driven carelessly because you were angry or frustrated or simply in a rush?

When was the last time you were unkind and dismissive to your children or loved ones because you were in a bad mood, suffering a headache, or experiencing an agonizing disappointment at work?

When was the last time you lied because you feared the consequences if the complete truth was known? How long has it been since you lost your temper, became disrespectful, or expressed serious impatience with someone? When was your arrogance on full display? When did your propensity for exaggerating facts rear its head?

Such questions are a test, forcing us to examine our character strength. If we pass the test, it means our muscle strength is adequate for the challenge. If we fail, the capacity of our moral muscles is exceeded and needs some work.

Let's look at the emissions cheating scandal at Volkswagen, one of countless examples of corporate immorality and unethical behavior. From 2009 to 2015, Volkswagen intentionally programmed turbo-charged diesel engines to emit 40 times less nitrogen oxide (NO_x) in emissions testing compared to emissions in real-world driving. When this fraudulent activity was discovered, the company became the target of a criminal investigation in several countries. Volkswagen's stock fell dramatically. Martin Winterkorn, Group CEO, resigned. In April 2017, Volkswagen agreed to pay a $2.8 billion criminal fine for deliberately cheating on emissions tests.

The decision to cheat was probably made by just a few leaders but the entire company and its shareholders suffered the embarrassment and the cost. Whatever pressures existed for those executives who crossed moral boundaries, the capacity of their moral muscles was exceeded.

THE GRADUAL NUMBING OF MORAL MUSCLES

If you love going faster than the speed limit, this example should resonate.

Fred had a 40-minute commute to and from work each day, most of it on open highway. For years, he rarely drove his car more than five miles per hour over the speed limit; his strongest deterrent was the fear of a speeding ticket. The turning point in Fred's driving habits came one day when he was running behind for a critical appointment at work. Instead of going only 5 mph over the speed limit, Fred sped along at 15–20 mph over. Fred made his meeting, his commute was less boring – and he didn't get a ticket.

Fred now drives well over the speed limit almost all the time, sometimes by 30 mph over. He is acutely aware of his frustration with slow drivers, even those going the speed limit. He honks his horn and tailgates those who won't move over from the passing lane.

In the last two years, Fred has received two speeding tickets, but rather than reducing his driving speed, he installed multiple sophisticated radar detection systems in his car. "Everyone speeds," says Fred. "Some go much faster than I do. I'm tempted to go faster, but I hold myself back." Rather than being calm upon arrival at work or at home, Fred is often edgy and irritated, mostly because of "stupid drivers out there." Despite the increased risk of hurting others by his speeding, Fred feels he has crossed no moral line. This is about getting to his destination on time and minimizing travel boredom – that's it. His moral sensitivities are not moved by his intentional, illegal act of speeding, which increases the risk of harming others. Put another way, the moral muscles that should be engaged by Fred's behavior have become numb, inoperable.

The moral transgression of speeding – or jaywalking, or rounding off numbers on one's taxes, or occasionally fudging the truth at work, or a host of other seemingly "victimless" crimes – may seem so commonplace, so accepted, so *slight*, that even to examine them seems silly. But could moral numbing at the smaller levels – indeed, at any level – help to explain why so many leaders failed to raise red flags when confronted with much more serious moral abuses, like those that led to the 2007–2008 financial crisis? When we look around and see everyone crossing the same moral line, when no one appears to be getting seriously, permanently hurt – at least not yet – and when there is a potential positive payoff for playing the game by the new rules, is it not expedient and downright common sense to "turn off" or numb the moral muscles involved? Could this leap partly explain the behavior of

Raheem Brennerman, CEO of Blacksands Pacific Group, who reportedly defrauded financial institutions of what eventually added up to more than $300 million, leading to federal charges in 2017 of bank fraud, wire fraud, and conspiracy? Brennerman was accused of using ill-gotten loans to purchase personal real estate, jewelry, travel, and spa treatments. What was he thinking? What thought process legitimized this behavior? When moral muscles are numbed, nearly any aberrant behavior becomes acceptable.

According to social psychologist Peter Ditto, "motivated reasoning" is the tendency to cherry-pick facts that support conclusions and beliefs we're vested in maintaining. The facts are the facts, but we ignore, alter, or otherwise twist them to allow us to continue doing what we're doing. Once we learn we can get what we want by altering the logic chain, by embracing "facts" that align with the outcome we want and dismissing those facts that don't, no behavior is safe. No value, no belief is safe. Was it motivated reasoning that resulted in the 2016 criminal charges against six executives of INSYS Therapeutics for participating in a scheme to bribe doctors to prescribe a highly addictive, fentanyl-based painkiller? One of the executives was accused of directing employees to claim a fraudulent cancer diagnosis for patients, to better meet insurance company reimbursement guidelines. How utterly contorted must one's "logic chain" get to behave in this criminal, immoral way? The facts that supported the executives' decision to bribe doctors and falsely meet insurance guidelines must have been embraced; those facts that didn't were ignored. Did motivated reasoning contribute to the 2007–2008 meltdown? To what extent does this tendency contribute to our own moral failures, small and large?

Researchers Ann Tenbrunsel and David Messick contend that one of the chief factors in unethical behavior is self-deception, which leads to a phenomenon they term "ethical fading." In the journal *Social Justice Research*, they write: "Self-deception allows one to behave self-interestedly while, at the same time, falsely believing that one's moral principles were upheld. The result of this internal con game is that the ethical aspects of the decision 'fade' into the background, the moral implications obscured." They argue that ethics training in organizations is doomed to limited success so long as course designers fail to acknowledge the psychological propensity of employees toward (unconscious) self-deception – the lies we tell ourselves and the secrets we keep from ourselves, which enables a range of unethical decisions and behaviors. Self-deception blurs ethical reality to such an extent that our moral sensibilities, at least about the given issue, are dormant. Ethical considerations fade from conscious reach.

To what extent did ethical fading play a role in Deborah Kelley's corporate misconduct? The former managing director of Sterne Agee, a brokerage firm, admitted that between 2014 and 2016, she paid bribes to the director of a fixed-income retirement fund in exchange for his steering business to her firm. According to prosecutors, Kelley received 35–40% of hundreds of thousands of dollars in commissions from trades that the firm "earned." What type of internal con game, what type of self-deception, allowed her to formulate the plan, pay the bribes, receive the commissions – and somehow *still* believe her moral principles were upheld? To what extent did ethical fading play a role in the 2007–2008 financial crisis and to what extent has it contributed to ethical failures of our own?

IMPOSTER SYNDROME

Another persistent problem among today's leaders may not at first seem to stem from a character deficit – yet it highlights how failure to develop moral muscles can result in self-sabotage and character vulnerability, which can corrode one's ability as a leader and human being.

The issue is Imposter Syndrome, the term coined in 1978 by clinical psychologists Pauline Clance and Suzanne Imes: that belief that you are inadequate and/or undeserving of your role or success, and that it's only a matter of time before others will find out and expose you as a fraud. Almost everyone experiences Imposter Syndrome at some point – even the most successful global CEOs and C-suite executives. Instead of feeling the joy and accomplishment that they expected when reaching the top, many CEOs feel lonely, anxious, and vulnerable – as if they're failing in both their corporate role as well as their relationships with the people who matter most to them. Entrepreneurs can be especially vulnerable as they chart uncertain territory and often lack the skills and years of experience of more seasoned leaders. For each leader who first achieves the level of CEO or equivalent, there can be feelings of *Why would they listen to me? What if they found out I didn't have the experience they did? What if my vision doesn't pan out?* (Interestingly, while early research on this syndrome focused on high-achieving women, it's been found to affect men and women about equally.)

Leaders who experience Imposter Syndrome are not by definition unethical, or even noticeably morally deficient; they are not necessarily the type of leader who so obviously fails in important character ways (e.g., encourages winning at all costs, believes fear is a better motivator than kindness, fosters mistrust in the company's culture to increase paranoia, ergo to – in his/her mind – increase productivity, etc.).

So why do we include such types here?

Because it's not just character development that has changed somewhat in our current world; it's also the nature of leadership. Leaders are now continuously in the spotlight, facing ever-greater demands and expected to possess an expanded set of competencies, to take a stance on social and political issues, and to navigate complexity – all while needing to continuously disrupt themselves and their organizations. We evolve business processes, business models, technology at lightning speed – yet fail to evolve the human beings who are at the core and required to make all of this successful. Leaders who struggle with Imposter Syndrome – virtually all leaders, actually – often feel stressed, anxious, and overwhelmed. Ongoing fear of being exposed is associated with higher levels of the stress hormone cortisol in the brain and body, and with higher levels of anxiety and depression. Feelings of insecurity can cause one to work even harder and neglect self-care (eating well, engaging in physical activity, getting enough quality sleep and regular recovery, etc.) and turn to unhealthy behavior and even substance abuse. Imposter Syndrome and lack of confidence may also limit one's willingness to take risks and to be creative, agile, and disruptive – all key attributes of a successful entrepreneur and business leader.

There's yet *another* reason we highlight Imposter Syndrome: Self-doubt often results in a lack of trust and confidence in others, and research suggests that this can impact decision-making and ethical standards. When we experience self-doubt, we not only judge ourselves critically, but are more likely to judge others critically, which can impact our ability to build strong, healthy, and productive relationships. Additionally, those who struggle with Imposter Syndrome often feel they can never really let people know who they are, because in their mind they are a fraud. This can cause others to perceive them as very distant and difficult to know, which can undermine trust and team spirit.

Not exactly an environment of character *or* leadership.

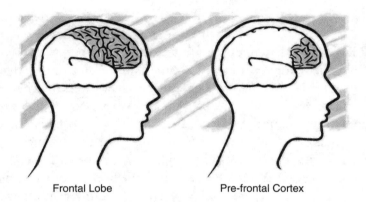

Frontal Lobe   Pre-frontal Cortex

WE RESIST EXAMINING THE CONSEQUENCES

Two regions of our rational brain play a critical role in moral reasoning and decision-making: the frontal lobe and the pre-frontal cortex. Taken together, they equip us to project the possible future consequences of our choices. Abstract thinking, thought analysis, planning, decision-making, and an array of other executive functions – these all become possible with this evolutionary upgrade. This neurological architecture gifts us the ability to look into the future with such vividness and seeming clarity that powerful emotions flow upon conjuring that future. The simple act of imagining how we would feel, say, if our son or daughter were killed in a car crash triggers surprisingly "real" feelings of grief, sadness, horror. Our ability to predict the negative consequence if we were to pursue a particular course of action represents a remarkable capability. We don't have to wait to go through a protracted divorce because of an affair before we can understand how that affair, theoretically, could very well lead to that traumatic result. We don't have to first get fired because we crossed ethical lines to predict how such a transgression could well lead to termination of our employment, how it would likely affect our future job prospects and our family's, and how terribly it would make us feel. We don't have to actually hurt someone while driving intoxicated to project how mortified and devastated we would feel were it actually to happen.

Do you think Lee Iacocca, the legendary auto executive and EVP of Ford Motor Company during the launch of the infamous Pinto, would have immediately called for a redesign had he projected how a leaky fuel tank could explode into flames and result in more than two dozen deaths? Unfortunately, Iacocca was never given the chance: He wasn't informed about the leaks until it was too late. Some employees apparently *did* know, however, as the result of a cost-benefit analysis (known as the "Pinto Memo") that weighed the potential loss of human life with the cost of manufacturing delays, and deemed the delays too expensive. Would Barry Bonds, the home-run-slugging outfielder for the San Francisco Giants, have made different choices had he carefully considered the possibility of indictment for illegally using steroids, and the permanent stain to his reputation as an athlete and a person? If Dennis Kozlowski, former CEO of Tyco International, had truly and carefully projected the potential consequences of his actions, knowing that they could well lead to criminal conviction and extended jail time – and did – would he have made different choices? Sam Waksal, former CEO of ImClone Systems, was convicted of several securities violations, and as a consequence served time in federal prison . . . if he had used his power of projection, which we human beings are blessed to possess, would he have elected not to cross moral lines? How about Kenneth Lay, former chairman of Enron, who was found guilty of 10 counts of securities fraud, or Bernie Madoff, who admitted to operating a Ponzi scheme that resulted in arguably the largest fraud in U.S. history?

Take a moment to consider your worst moral failures. How many bad choices have you made because you failed to consider the possible negative consequences for yourself and, more importantly, for others?

As just noted, we all possess the ability to extrapolate into the future and explore potential consequences. But because exploring the downside may prevent us from getting or doing what we want, we resist it. We continue forward, believing it's all going to work out okay. If we need to add a little denial or ignoring to the mix: So be it. The capacity we possess that could, if exercised, save the day for us is, all too often, put in lockdown. It represents just another example of how we numb our moral operating system.

We begin with seemingly benign breaches of our moral boundaries, and over time, it becomes easier and easier to get what we want and not feel guilty. One day we become shocked by how far we have drifted morally.

Researcher Dan Ariely, professor of psychology and behavioral economics at Duke University, contends that our behavior is fundamentally driven by two opposing motivations:

1. We want to view ourselves as possessing good moral character.

2. We want to benefit as much as possible from taking short cuts – better known as cheating.

We ask ourselves (almost always quietly, often unconsciously): How far can I go into questionable moral territory before my sensibilities perk up and I begin feeling bad or guilty about what I'm doing? How many moral lines – or which moral lines – can I cross and still feel good about myself? How much can I cheat on my taxes, on my golf scorecard, on tests; how fast can I drive above the speed limit, how many times can I refuse to confront corruption; how much can I do all of that and *still* qualify as a good person in my own eyes? How much less than maximally trustworthy, kind, compassionate, and caring can I be and still qualify?

Each person's morality system operates within boundaries that define acceptable and unacceptable behavior. It might be useful to think of morality as a circle. The behavior occurring inside the circle is morally right and acceptable; outside the circle is wrong and unacceptable. Great variations exist both in the size of morality circles and in the permeability of their circumferences. A small circle means we have little room for moral maneuvering; a large circle, more. The permeability of the circumference – the boundary – correlates to the rigidity or flexibility of the moral tenets contained within the circle. For example, my sister is a Catholic nun, which suggests a small circle (little room to maneuver morally) and an impermeable boundary (core tenets are mostly fixed). Bernie Madoff's behavior suggests a large circle with a very porous boundary.[2]

---

[2]A small circle with a porous boundary might represent a child with a very rigid morality system who is always getting into trouble. A large circle with a barely porous boundary might represent a libertarian who seeks maximum freedom and autonomy but is skeptical of authority and state power.

The boundary of the circle is the moral barrier we use to judge whether our behavior is right or wrong. When the boundary is breached, painful feelings of guilt, shame, or remorse often follow . . . but not necessarily! We deploy a variety of ingenious methods to dismantle our guilt/remorse system, thus supporting what Ariely calls our "fudge factor": the ability to do immoral things (e.g., cheating) while still feeling good about ourselves.

Acting morally is not a sometime goal. It is an all-the time goal.

A core objective of this book is to equip leaders with the tools necessary to determine both the size and permeability of their moral circles.

The two principal tools to help you identify those two factors, and also to reverse the numbing process, motivated reasoning, and ethical fading are:

1. Increased awareness

2. The creation and deployment of a Personal Credo

Before we explore these tools, a question: What do moral lapses away from work – such as driving while intoxicated, cheating in golf or on exams, being rude or dismissive with family members, losing our temper with a waiter, customer service representative, or post office employee, and so forth – have to do with our ability to lead with character at work?

Answer: everything! Moral strengths and weaknesses apply to every dimension of our lives. Numbed moral muscles at home will likely manifest themselves at work, and vice versa. Your character is your character regardless of where you are or what you're doing. To lead with character means (among other things) that there is no distinction between your moral character at home or at work. Decisions that move the moral needle backward at home will likely manifest (directly or indirectly) at work. To lead with character is to maintain the highest possible standard of moral excellence wherever you are at the moment.

Another question: Should you, as a leader, choose as your moral default line an area close to the area that makes you feel guilty? In other words, is the idea to push and probe your moral limit to see what you can get away with? Is this the calculus you want to use to run your life, the system by which you determine right from wrong?

Of course not!

Ariely may have discovered that the moral line most people unknowingly choose is that which comes as close as possible to the "edge" and still allows them to feel good about themselves. But this book offers a vastly different approach to personal morality. In the chapters that follow, you learn how to intentionally, thoughtfully craft a document called a Personal Credo. This replaces the What-can-I-get-away-with? moral calculus. The credo-building and -strengthening process build-in short 10-minute daily writing assignments spread over three months (with another recommended two months to fully habituate the energy and reflection you have invested). The daily process is designed to awaken your moral sensibilities, to reverse all forms of moral numbing, and to provide you, the leader, with a thoroughly vetted moral calculus for judging right from wrong. By following this template, your character will be clear, strong, and impenetrable by forces that will inevitably present themselves to tempt, weaken, or corrupt you. You will lead with character at work and at home. You will lead with character wherever you are, under any circumstance.

Character-building – identifying your core values and strengthening your character muscles – is a personal journey; in many ways, it's a solitary journey. If we were to embark on this journey by using another human being's character as the ideal, we would likely invite disappointment and disillusionment because, at some point, our very human hero is destined to stumble and fall. Women and men of even the highest character fail. Repeatedly. Often daily.

But they do not fail us; they fail themselves. Nor does their failure negate the absolute value of character. We are not gods. No mortal can ever be the ultimate example of character. (Although I have devoted a good percentage of my career exploring the issue of character, and I have presumed to write a book about it, in no way do I consider myself the exemplar of perfect character.)

So you needn't compare yourself with those whose characters you admire. In fact, you shouldn't.

On the other hand, beware not to fall into this common trap: "Hey, I may drive at dangerous speeds, be occasionally rude and dismissive to others, be frequently (but not always) arrogant and impatient . . . but I'm doing pretty damn well compared to Bernie Madoff, Kenneth Lay, Dennis Kozlowski, Elizabeth Holmes, Les Moonves, Mark McGwire, and so forth."

The ominous truth? Even small lapses in our moral character, if unchecked, can lead to unintentional, even tragic outcomes.

CHARACTER CALL-OUTS

For You   For Work   For Family

MORAL INTEGRITY

Definition: The acquired disposition to act in accordance with what you judge to be morally right (Moral Strength).

Self: To act with moral integrity is to act according to one's highest moral and ethical standards. Your actions are fully aligned with your core values and principles. At the end of each day, grade yourself on whether you actually did what you judged to be the right thing to do.

Others: (Business) Discuss what integrity means to your team and to your company. Explore how moral integrity is demonstrated by team members. Ask for concrete examples. Ask for examples in other companies where the moral integrity test was failed. What were the consequences? (Family) Discuss the importance of integrity to success in life as a person and as a family. Ask family members to give examples of integrity – how it is manifested in one's life and how it is not. This is a great time to explore core values.

Rate Yourself:

       1   2   3   4   5

Relatively Weak   Relatively Strong

CHARACTER CALL-OUTS

For You   For Work   For Family

MORAL COURAGE

Definition: The acquired disposition to act in accordance with what you believe is morally right despite any risk or negative consequences to you or to others (Moral Strength).

Self: Courage is foundational to being a person of strong character. It's important to understand that courage, like all character muscles, is an acquired capacity. The strength of this muscle enables you to keep fighting and investing energy regardless of the risks. Look for newspaper articles, magazine stories, movies such as *Act of Valor*, and so forth, and consider what changes must occur within yourself that would enable you to act so courageously. Find at least one situation each week to act in accordance with your values despite any risk or negative consequence. Keep a record.

Others: (Business) Discuss the role of moral courage in leadership. Ask your team questions like How does the muscle of courage manifest itself in a business environment? How often does one's job offer opportunities to strengthen this muscle? Explain how holding an ethical line or exposing corrupt practices requires courage. (Family) Discuss how standing up for what one believes in, protecting the rights of others, taking the road less traveled, and so forth can be powerful ways to strengthen courage. Have each family member report on one thing he or she did in the last two weeks that required moral courage.

Rate Yourself:

1	2	3	4	5
Relatively Weak				Relatively Strong

CHARACTER CALL-OUTS

For You   For Work   For Family

PERSONAL COURAGE

Definition: The acquired disposition to act in accordance with what you believe is the right thing to do despite any risks or negative consequences to you (Performance Strength).

Self: Like moral courage, personal courage is foundational to being a person of strong character. This is the strength required to push through doubts and fears and take a risk. Examples could be making a high-risk move in chess, going for a difficult shot under pressure in tennis, applying for another loan to grow your private business, or going for the automobile land speed record. Taking risks to learn a new habit, to master a new language, to go back to school and earn an advanced degree are also examples.

Others: (Business) Discuss the role personal courage plays in being a strong leader. Have team members give examples of personal courage in their business lives. How does risk taking and confronting personal fears contribute to business success? (Family) Discuss how courageously facing personal fears and doubts is at the core of being a successful person. Have family members provide one example of how courage was used to push through fears or doubts and do the right thing.

Rate Yourself:

1	2	3	4	5
Relatively Weak				Relatively Strong

Character Call-Outs

For You　　For Work　　For Family

SELF-CONTROL / WILLPOWER

Definition: The acquired disposition to mobilize the necessary energy to exercise restraint over one's impulses, desires, and emotions, and to fulfill one's intentions (Performance Strength).

Self: Pick one area of your life where exercising self-control is required to build a desired new habit (ritual). An example would be eating a healthy snack every two to four hours while working. Another might be to get up from your desk every 90 minutes and move for 3 to 5 minutes. Keep a detailed record of your self-control investment. Continue until the habit becomes fully formed.

Others: (Business) Encourage team members to provide examples of where they resisted impulses to act or say things that were not in the best interest of the business (either with external clients or with fellow team members). (Family) Encourage family members to give one example every week of where they delayed immediate gratification or exercised self-control to resist an impulse to do something that was not in their best interest.

Rate Yourself:

1	2	3	4	5
Relatively Weak				Relatively Strong

CHARACTER CALL-OUTS

For You   For Work   For Family

MOTIVATION

Definition: The acquired disposition to energize one's self to act (Performance Strength).

Self: Energizing oneself to act is a critical life skill. Motivating yourself to act begins by establishing a purpose for doing so. The more the purpose connects to important needs, the more likely you will move yourself to act. Winning the battle of procrastination and laziness is enhanced in goal setting that connects to important perceived needs that are intrinsically rather than extrinsically driven.

Others: (Business) Companies often bring motivational speakers in to fire up their employee base. The effect is usually very short-lived. The most powerful and enduring form of motivation is self-motivation. The ability to motivate oneself is a critical performance character strength. Self-motivation is most effective when it is intrinsic rather than extrinsic and links to important values and needs such as autonomy, competence, and connecting to others. Ask each team member to explain to the team what motivates him or her and how he or she stays motivated to do their work, day after day. (Family) Discuss the difference between intrinsic and extrinsic motivation. Relate to issues of enjoyment, passion, and excitement. Have each family member write a paragraph on the importance of staying motivated in life and practically how to do it.

Rate Yourself:

1   2   3   4   5

Relatively Weak   Relatively Strong

CHARACTER CALL-OUTS

For You   For Work   For Family

FOCUS

Definition: The acquired disposition to control one's attention (Performance Strength).

Self: Spend 3 minutes daily meditating on your breathing – breathing in and breathing out. The goal is to merge action and awareness in the present moment. When your mind wanders, gently bring your focus back to your breathing. Steady improvement will occur with practice.

Others: (Business) Make a rule that all computers, cell phones, and so forth be turned off and put away during meetings. As a leader, you want full engagement and total focus from everyone. In return for their compliance, you agree to keep all meetings to 45 minutes or less. (Family) Turn off all cell phones, pagers, TVs, and so forth during dinner. For the first 30 minutes after arriving home from work, give 100% of your best focused energy to your family. No multi-tasking, no talking or thinking about work. Absorb yourself completely in the lives of your family.

Rate Yourself:

| 1 | 2 | 3 | 4 | 5 |

Relatively Weak   Relatively Strong

CHAPTER 2

Why Good Leaders Are Vulnerable to Corruption: A Flawed Morality System

It is curious that physical courage should be so common in the world and moral courage so rare. —Mark Twain

Facing the truth about all the many and complex dimensions of our ethical character is no easy task. Most leaders fervently believe they are people of strong moral character. They believe themselves to be men or women full of integrity, honesty, respect for others, and on and on. Merely asking questions – innocent but probing questions – about a leader's morality can stir troubling feelings in him or her: dismay, defensiveness, resentment. Since we presume ourselves to be good at heart, any suggestion otherwise is fundamentally distressing – to the vast majority of us, anyway. When we are forced to defend our character, we feel as if we are fighting for our psychological survival. We are not going to surrender that ground without a fight.

THE DARK SIDE

We have all witnessed the enormous capacity for good that human beings possess. Unfortunately, we are also painfully aware of the enormous capacity for unspeakable evil that many human beings possess. To rally ourselves to meet the moral challenges we repeatedly face, and to understand what's at stake when we fail to rally ourselves, we need to confront the truth about our dark side.

Whenever and wherever character fails, the consequences – in business, law, politics, religion, marriage, parenting, medicine, war, you name it – can be tragic. One of the most renowned behavioral research experiments provides us with a disturbing view into the dark side of our humanity, and what we're capable of. Starting in 1961, Stanley Milgram, a Yale psychologist, conducted a series of tests, the results of which were published in 1963. Milgram was interested in exploring the issue of obedience to authority. He wanted to see how easy or hard it would be for people to harm others when ordered to do so by an authority figure (and when there was no consequence to them from the individual being harmed). Participants were instructed to administer an electric shock to a student they could see in another room, each time the student made a mistake; the "idea" was to see how this might accelerate the student's learning process. Each mistake warranted an increasing level of shock. Intensities of shock started at 15 volts and proceeded to a dangerous 450 volts. All the participants continued to administer shocks up to 300 volts, though it was within their power to refuse; two-thirds of participants still administered shocks at 450 volts.

It so happened that no real shocks were being felt by the students; they acted as if they were being shocked.

According to Milgram, almost everyone follows orders because they were given by an authority figure. Our willingness to obey is ingrained in us from our early childhood. In the article, "The Perils of Obedience," Milgram asserted that individuals obey when they believe the authority figure will assume responsibility for the consequences of the individual's actions ("agency theory"). Milgram's experiment, with minimal variation, has been repeated across a variety of cultures, yielding more or less similar results; in some of the newer studies, obedience rates were actually higher than Milgram's. In 2015, for example, a research team from Poland replicated Milgram's study and discovered that little had changed in the last half-century. As reported in *Social Psychological and Personality Science*, the researchers found that *90%* of participants were willing to administer what they believed was the *highest* level of shock.

Milgram's research sends ominous messages: We can easily become indifferent to the suffering of others. We can be seduced into crossing critical moral lines simply by a manipulation of our external environment.

Easily modified factors such as peer pressure and conformity dynamics can overwhelm our moral defenses.

In a 1939 speech, Edwin Sutherland, president of the American Sociological Society, astonished his fellow sociologists by arguing that the most serious crimes in our society were committed by well-known, highly respected business leaders! His evidence? He had studied 70 large firms over several years and found that every single one of them had at least one civil or criminal decision against it. According to his findings, 60 of the 70 firms were found guilty in criminal court, with an average of four convictions each. In his 1949 book, *White Collar Crime*, Sutherland stated that seemingly ideal business leaders, as well as the large corporations they ran, were very much like professional thieves.

More than a quarter of the executives surveyed said they would use their professional discretion to make accounting adjustments to hit their desired earnings target.—Eugene Soltes, author of *Why They Do It*

The question, then, is this: Who are these people who fill the business news of today and the recent past with scandals, corrupt practices, and corporate misconduct? Who are these people who fall from grace, who willfully hurt others, who bribe, embezzle, cheat, misrepresent and manipulate the truth, who defraud, who intentionally violate safety measures, and on and on and on? According to Dean Ludwig and Clinton Longenecker, writing in the early 1990s in the *Journal of Business Ethics*, "The majority were of strong personal integrity and intelligence, individuals who have climbed the ladder through hard work and 'keeping their noses clean.' But just at the moment of seemingly 'having it all,' they seemed to throw it all away by engaging in an activity which is wrong, which they knew was wrong, which if it would be discovered would lead to their downfall, and which they mistakenly believed they had the power to conceal."

Who are these people who fall from grace? They are us.

We are *all* vulnerable to moral collapse. Perhaps Alexander Solzhenitsyn captures it best:

If only there were evil people somewhere insidiously committing evil deeds and it were necessary only to separate them from the rest of us and destroy them. But the line dividing good and evil cuts through the heart of every human being and who is willing to destroy a piece of his own heart?

THE MACHINERY OF MORALITY

Morality involves two things: determining the right thing to do, and then actually doing it.

Simply knowing the right action to take does not make us more virtuous. Knowing and doing originate from different operating systems, so knowing what's right does not automatically translate into doing what's right. In *Why They Do It*, Harvard Business School professor Eugene Soltes writes, "Professional ethicists behave no better than other similarly educated professionals . . . in some cases, their behavior was noticeably worse." Citing the research of Eric Schwitzgebel and Joshua Rust, Soltes notes the discrepancy between sophistication in moral judgment and behavior. It is this discrepancy that moral integrity addresses. That is, moral integrity is *the* core strength that enables us to act in accordance with what we judge to be morally right. Without moral integrity, our ability to live an ethical and moral life simply ceases. Because of this, moral integrity represents a whopping 50% of our moral character. Why do I say 50%? Let's keep it simple. 50% is determining the right thing to do; the remaining 50% is doing it.

We all struggle in getting both parts of morality right. Some examples:

- I know I shouldn't have said what I did, but I said it anyway.
- I know I should have listened, been respectful, and waited until she was finished speaking, but I interrupted and cut her off because I can't stand to hear her talk.

- I have no clue what the right thing is to do here, so I'm going to do nothing.

- I know I should tell him the truth, but I could not make myself do it.

- I sometimes do what I want even though I know it's not the right thing to do.

- I know I should have told the officer that I was the one who ran the red light, but I lied and accused the other driver of causing the accident.

Both integrity and moral integrity enable us to do what we judge to be the right thing. In order to actually to *do* the right thing, though, how much willpower do we need? Clearly, we need a developed sense of self-control and mental strength to complete the deal. In their 2011 book, *Willpower: Rediscovering the Greatest Human Strength*, Roy Baumeister and John Tierney, drawing on their own research and nearly 100 studies, argued that willpower works like a muscle, and that regular "exercise" boosts its strength. Willpower, Baumeister and Tierney contend, can be used to build character. Willpower draws down mental energy; that is, it's a limited resource. They say that factors that undermine energy production, such as low glucose levels and lack of sleep, cause "ego depletion." Some critics challenge this idea, citing inadequate sample size and "replication bias" (bias to support original findings). Regardless of whether Baumeister and Tierney's ego depletion construct is confirmed to be valid, it is clear that integrity is linked to willpower and self-control.

For nearly three decades at our Institute, we have helped individuals make significant life changes by controlling their energy production through improvements in nutritional intake, sleep, hydration, movement, and so forth. These are all important. If you don't take care of these inputs, you greatly increase the chance that your decision-making will suffer – decisions at work and at home, decisions that affect performance and moral character. But the greatest predictor of successful change, the "x factor" most likely to rally willpower, is purpose. That is, nothing is more important to making successful change than being motivated to do so; than having a deeply felt sense of personal purpose. In our experience, we discovered that the more that participants linked their desired change to their core values and a purpose bigger than themselves, the greater the probability that sufficient willpower would be rallied to support successful change; for instance, when your purpose is to be a better father, it becomes easier to get up and work out early in the morning to have more energy and engagement with your kids. Put another way, the more that "doing the right thing" could be linked to a deeply felt purpose beyond the individual's self-interest, the likelier it was that they would recruit the moral strength needed to do it. When doing the right thing on behalf of others involves risk to your or others' safety or well-being, the character strength of moral courage is called upon. Examples would be soldiers in battle; refusing to tell falsehoods about a competitor's product, at the risk of losing your job; telling the truth about safety violations you have witnessed and risking being demoted or worse (e.g., calling out O-ring hazards in the *Challenger* space shuttle disaster; whistleblowing Boeing and FAA failures in overseeing the 737 Max); calling out immoral behavior among comrades (e.g., New York City police officer Frank Serpico revealing widespread corruption in the police force; major-league pitcher Mike Fiers whistleblowing about the Houston Astros' sign-stealing); speaking out to save the lives of others despite threats to one's career or well-being (e.g., Dr. Li Wenliang, the Chinese physician who tried to warn others about the deadly coronavirus/COVID-19 and then died from the virus), and so forth. Moral integrity, willpower, moral courage, and purpose are intimately bound together. All can be strengthened with training.

USING SHAME TO DEMONSTRATE THE TWO ARMS OF MORALITY

Shame is part of the machinery of morality. It is deep distress caused by doing something you regret, painfully. It's a built-in punishment system designed to deter us from engaging in that activity in the future and, more generally, from straying outside ethical boundaries.

Let's try something, even though it will likely be uncomfortable.

Recall something in your life that produced deep shame or guilt, something that represents a clear failure of your morality system. As you look at it now, was it a failure of your moral judgment, such as publicly accusing someone of dishonesty that later proved to be untrue and had negative consequences for the accused? Or a failure to act in accordance with your moral compass – that is, your judgment was correct (e.g., having an affair with a co-worker is wrong) but you failed to act accordingly?

The case will be made in this chapter that both examples of moral failure can be traced to one or more of the following factors:

1. Flawed inputs

2. Lack of awareness

3. Weak muscles of ethical character (which form the basis of our Personal Credo)

POTENTIAL FLAWED INPUTS

The question of how our ethical system gets formed is a fascinating one. Multiple factors, many outside our control, can negatively influence our sense of right and wrong. Flawed moral inputs can be likened to faulty coding in a computer program. As with faulty software, coding flaws embedded in our morality system must be identified and addressed for the system to function properly. When considering how each of the following inputs applies to you, make every effort to take an honest, non-defensive look. Beware of internal stories that develop as you enter into uncomfortable territory (e.g., "This is a waste of time" or "I have enough stress in my life – shut this inquiry down"). An important resource to tap for accessing our truth is our built-in "crap detector." (Ernest Hemingway is credited with coining the phrase.) This "tool" helps us recognize that, in many circumstances, what we say publicly or privately does not in fact represent the real or whole truth. We acknowledge that what we are saying is a con, an exaggeration, a partial truth, maybe even a complete fabrication. Our Inner Voice calls us out. *You're spinning. You're making stuff up. You're hiding from the truth.* That voice, when properly trained, can aid us whenever and wherever moral issues are involved. If this voice is *not* trained, then it grows dangerously silent. By failing to recognize its value, we naturally fail to nourish it, and soon we don't have access to it. And once this voice, this crucial broadcaster of our "crap detector," has been turned off, leading with character is no longer attainable.

We are marvelous in many ways, but the moral laws within us are a mixed blessing.—Joshua Greene

Various flawed inputs that influence character include the following.

Fake News and Moral Reasoning

Fake news is not just a problem in politics; it's a contaminant in our moral lives, as well. In the political sense, fake news refers to news that's been tainted to support an ideology. Facts are selectively woven together to bolster a biased narrative and presented as unvarnished truth. It occurs throughout the political spectrum. When readers expect straight-up, fact-based reporting but realize they're getting news designed to influence their politics, they feel cheated and used. Unfortunately, unsuspecting consumers of news can find their opinions and beliefs shifting in the direction of the biased input when fake news is successfully, voluminously masqueraded as real news. That's the intent behind deceptive news reporting. When the same politically slanted "facts" are presented in an opinion piece, we're much less likely to be seduced by the commentator's narrative because we know the conclusions presented are colored by that person's biases. Importantly, when we judge incoming information to be legitimately fact-based, our "crap detector" is less likely to be alerted.

Unfortunately, this dynamic happens not only with politics but with moral reasoning, too. When our personal beliefs and biases masquerade as factual knowledge – that is, as a form of internal fake news whose factuality is more dubious than we suspect – our critical, questioning voice remains dormant, which compromises our moral reasoning (e.g., you fail to question your belief that going to the bar for a drink will not be a problem). Similar to news about our world, where facts ought to be distinguished from opinion, in our own life and our own circle it's crucial to distinguish objective truth from our personal beliefs and wants. Fake news in any form is a flawed input that can corrupt our thinking morally, just as it may do so politically.

Flawed Parental Inputs

When we poll clients who attend our programs at the Institute, the overwhelming majority report that the greatest single influence on their sense of right and wrong was their parents, and most readers of this book likely feel the same. Perhaps the greatest gift is to be blessed with parents who are models of extraordinary moral character.

The inevitable question, though: Do parents ever get it wrong morally? The answer, of course, is Yes! Are they not human? Deficiencies in kindness, humility, gratitude, patience, compassion, integrity, and so forth, can be found in our parents – yours, mine, everyone's. Our parents were or are imperfect. And just as they hand down to us their character strengths, they also hand down their character flaws, though usually unintentionally. Consider for a moment whether your ethical flaws are like those of your parents – for instance, you tend to withdraw love as a manipulation to get what you want; you are condescending to those less financially fortunate. To what extent do these same issues surface in your corporate life – for instance, you are always respectful to superiors but not necessarily to those below you on the corporate ladder. If this is so, have you found a way to correct them?

Also: Are your character traits a *reaction* to your parent's flaws?

Flawed Cultural Inputs

Culture reflects the attitudes and behavior of a social group. Do you think the culture of a country club or a street gang influences its members' sense of right and wrong? How about the group you hung out with when you were developing? Was the subculture you experienced as a teenager and young adult supportive and nurturing, providing a strong and healthy moral foundation? What was your peer group's attitude about sex, cheating, violence, social responsibility, and moral-ity, in general? How significant was the influence of your peers on your current character as a corporate leader? Note that we're not searching for excuses when we examine potential sources of faulty moral coding; we're looking to increase our understanding and awareness of poten-tially contaminating influences, so we can better address them.

Of course, as profound an influence as our environment has on us when we are young, we are not immune to influences as adults or even as leaders in our community. Think about your current culture, and your sub-culture of friends, neighbors, in-laws, and so forth. Consider the culture of the organization you represent.

Go smaller: Consider the culture of your department, business unit, or team. On the scale of importance, where are traits like integrity, hon-esty, generosity, humility, respect for others, loyalty, and compassion? In the culture(s) where you now find yourself, do ethical character strengths take a back seat to performance character strengths like ambition, com-petitiveness, and resilience?

Flawed Religious Inputs

Groups who attend our training programs consistently rank religious inputs as the second most powerful influence on the formation of their character, just behind parental inputs. We tend to believe religious influ-ences will have a largely positive effect on moral character development, and in many and profound instances, that's the case. But is it always?

I come from a strong religious background. I attended a Catholic elementary school, four years of Jesuit high school, and four years of Jesuit college. As I wrote earlier, my sister is a nun, and my brother studied for seven years to be a Jesuit priest before deciding to leave. My mother and father were both deeply religious, especially my mom. For them, nearly everything that happened in our lives, good and bad, was tied to Catholic teachings. For Mom, the origin of all truth came from her religious beliefs, and her mission in life was to convert as many people as possible to Catholicism. I remember listening to her, over and over, denounce other religions and especially non-believers. Although her tone softened as she got older, I remember (how could I ever forget this?) her insisting to me, when I was a young boy, that "transgressions" like eating meat on Fridays, missing Sunday mass, or having impure thoughts – if continued – would result in an eternity in hell. Those who knew her would freely attest to Mom's goodness, her deep caring for others, and her strength of character. These same people would also caution you not to tangle with her religious beliefs. As Mom grew older, she became increasingly concerned about radical violent Islam. For her, the fundamental problem with the Muslim religion was simply that they were not followers of Jesus Christ. I recall a discussion where she insisted that Muslims needed to convert or be eliminated from the Earth. I asked her, "If you could eliminate all Muslims from the Earth with the single push of a button, would you?" After a brief pause, she said, "Yes. I would be doing God's will." The following morning, Mom said that, after reflection, she definitely would *not* push the button. Still, this vividly shows how, despite religion's great power to enhance moral character, inflexible religious beliefs have the potential to compromise our moral reasoning in a deeply disturbing way.

How many wars have been fought and lives lost due to "nothing more than" conflicting religious beliefs? Many of the greatest atrocities in human history, including the killing of women, children, and civilians generally, and torture, have been perpetrated in the name of religion. All too often, the mindset of those committing the heinous acts is that they were divinely inspired.

How is it that, with so many years of religious and moral training, such a considerable percentage of Catholic priests could be found guilty of sexually abusing countless children worldwide, over decades? *Centuries?* At least as troubling and arguably more so, how could church leaders – people who also went through rigorous religious and moral training and who, for one reason or another, rose to a level of great moral and executive authority and power – knowingly cover up such atrocities, and in many ways guarantee that they continue against new waves of defenseless victims? The alarming but obvious answer: Even the most holy among us are vulnerable to moral collapse.

My point here is not to bash or even mildly denigrate religion or religious beliefs. I am certain that my own religious upbringing helped to form my moral character in a profoundly positive way. But there are two crucial takeaways. First, although most religious teachings are supportive of strong moral character, not all are. Second, being exposed to years of religious teachings does not, in and of itself, prevent moral collapse.

Flawed Mindset Inputs

There is reality – and then there's our version of reality. The two may be vastly different. My version of reality is "my story." My story represents the real world to me and dictates how I will respond in a given situation. Ethics researchers Ann Tenbrunsel and David Messick describe the embedded flaw: "We are creative narrators of stories that tend to allow us to do what we want and that justify what we have done."

Many psychologists, particularly Carol Dweck, refer to this as "mindset." Researchers have repeatedly demonstrated the power that mindset has to influence behavior. Suppose our mindset insists to us that, hey, *everyone* in business cuts corners and crosses moral lines; that businesses can't succeed if some moral lines are not crossed; that most leaders are selfish; that kindness and compassion are weaknesses; and on and on. Such beliefs represent glitches (coding errors) in our moral mindset. Yet we're unaware of the faultiness of these beliefs, or we have constructed a worldview where they simply *must* be true. Because we are convinced that such beliefs represent reality, we don't challenge their veracity. Unfortunately, we all have them and they all weaken our character in some way.

Flawed Emotional Inputs

We've all experienced times when our moral judgment has been blinded by emotion, when intense feelings of rage, anger, jealousy, envy, and so forth, hijack our ability to do what we know is right. Clearly our moral processing system can become seriously degraded with the intrusion of powerful emotions. Another glitch!

Flawed Survival Inputs

Does our moral calculus – specifically, our treatment of others – change when we're in "survival mode"? When we're under intense pressure, when we fear failure or humiliation, when we're facing a "fight or flight" threat? What happens to our concern for others, to our ability to be compassionate, kind, fair, honest, and respectful? Intense fear for our own well-being can be a formidable contaminant in our moral processing.

Flawed Fatigue Inputs

To what extent does hunger (from low blood sugar), lack of sleep, little or no exercise, and so forth impact our treatment of others? In this compromised physical (and mental) state, what happens to our commitment to show patience, to be loving, caring, humble, and so forth? What's the impact on our moral reasoning and judgment as leaders? It should be obvious by now that fatigue can crash our moral system in a significant way. One more agonizing programming glitch!

Flawed Need Inputs

How do strong needs for approval, attention, recognition, love, affection, self-esteem, and so forth impact our moral compass? Are we more likely to be drawn to the dark side when we are psychologically needy and feeling deficient? Are we likelier to seek comfort through alcohol, drugs, illicit sex, and so forth? Think back to a time when you seriously breached an important moral line. How psychologically needy were you at the time? Did your neediness perhaps cloud your judgment or your ability to act on your judgment?

You are not right because people agree with you; you are right because your facts and reasoning are right.

All the coding flaws just reviewed fundamentally blind us from the truth – or at least a truer picture of reality. Reality is distorted by compromised data, and since our very human coding flaws compromise us, the conclusions we draw are often distorted, skewed, shortsighted. Human beings shut down critical sources of input by blocking awareness. We can't consider that which we are not aware of; we block inputs so that they won't interfere with our current biases, which we believe are serving us quite nicely. Rather than pursuing a fact-based, unbiased inquiry into the soundness of our moral calculus, we consider only those facts that support what we really want to believe; and block out (disregard or discredit) facts that are unsupportive of those beliefs. Our conscious brain acts not unlike a defense attorney defending a client: It challenges evidence that does not support the conclusion we wish to be reached; we build a biased logic trail that does.

And this all occurs, for the most part, outside of our awareness.

A Personal Credo is an intentionally crafted ethical and moral document that essentially becomes, after deep and exhaustive reflection, the ultimate source code for any ethical or moral deliberation.

The Voices of Morality

Our brain consists of two built-in "advisory" voices: We consult them when determining the morally right thing to do.

The first voice comes from an intuitive processor, referred to as "System 1" by psychologist and bestselling author Daniel Kahneman. System 1 operates automatically and instinctively, and for the most part, unconsciously. This is our gut response. Inputs to this processor are vast and complex, stemming all the way back to earliest childhood. This voice of counsel is quick and capable of producing instantaneous and intense emotions, positive and negative. The feelings range from disgust to attraction, fear to deep trust, and they can begin registering immediately. Just looking at someone's face or walking into a room of strangers can produce an instant gut response. When we're asked to explain why we feel the way we do, we may have trouble giving a logical answer. The reason? The intuitive processor operates outside our ordinary consciousness and doesn't follow step-by-step, reasoned analysis.

The second built-in advisory voice, referred to by Kahneman as "System 2," is one we *can* consult, though it takes considerably more time to come to a definitive answer. That's because it emanates from our cognitive processor, which uses logical analysis and fact-crunching to render its moral decision. Although our rational and emotional brains are linked in important ways, this processor seeks the unvarnished truth about the ethical choices facing it, stripped clean of biasing emotion. Most of its operations are done consciously; before any decision is rendered, consultation with an array of sources usually takes place. Those sources include core beliefs, core values, and any intentionally developed moral operating documents, such as a Personal Credo.

A Personal Credo is an intentionally crafted document that becomes, after deep and exhaustive reflection, the source code for any moral deliberation. An important component of our credo is the strength of specific moral muscles that form the neurological machinery for judging and then doing the right thing. Strong muscles of kindness, compassion, honesty, gratitude, humility, integrity, and so forth represent the building blocks of our Personal Credo, and should weigh heavily in all moral decisions we make and actions we take.

WHICH VOICE IS THE BEST ADVISOR?

If our gut reaction to stimuli were a more reliable source of wisdom compared to our reflective, slower, cognitive approach, things would be much easier. But it's not. Sound judgment requires both systems to be activated and fully functional; and, in fact, as is shown by our experience at the Institute, as well as by research by Harvard's Joshua Greene and others, we should – time permitting – *lead* moral inquiry with the cognitive system. That means discounting our gut response for a period of time – shutting it off. At the Institute, we encourage our clients to consult their well-fortified, intentionally constructed Personal Credo, which consciously, deliberately establishes a hierarchy of values and a highest purpose in life.

Armed with this document, we can best examine the facts, conflicts, consequences, and choices that stand before us. Next, we summon our more deliberative empathy-compassion-kindness circuit and see where our heart takes us. Third and last in the process, we summon our intuitive response, listening carefully to what our gut is telling us.

Once these three sources of input are considered, a decision can be consciously rendered, with the highest priority afforded to our cognitive system because it has been carefully and thoroughly pre-loaded with our deepest purpose and most cherished values.

This book seeks to move the moral operating principles contained in one's Personal Credo from deliberative and conscious (System 2) to reflective and intuitive (System 1), with intentional daily training. Many moral decisions must be made with little or no time for conscious reflection. The training program detailed in this book provides for this.

After going through the numerous sources of input that may potentially hijack our moral character, examining how readily our moral reasoning and judgment can be undermined, then looking at how vulnerable both of our processor systems (intuitive and cognitive) are to being corrupted, you may be left wondering: How do we *ever* win the battle to do the right thing? The forces we're up against can be daunting. Our experience has taught us that the best chance that leaders have to meet the inevitable moral challenges they face daily is to commit to continuous training in three areas:

1. Confront and address the flaws in their moral operating system.

2. Work to raise their ethical awareness, so that we may better combat the ingenious ways we distort reality to get what we want.[1]

3. Strengthen their ethical muscles, because they represent the central core of our Personal Credo.

At the heart of science is an essential balance between two seemingly contradictory attitudes – an openness to new ideas, no matter how bizarre or counterintuitive they may be, and the most ruthless scrutiny of ideas, old and new. This is how deep truths are winnowed from deep nonsense.—Carl Sagan

[1]For a list of the ways our moral reasoning and judgment can be corrupted, see Appendix B.

CHARACTER CALL-OUTS

For You   For Work   For Family

JUSTICE

Definition: The acquired disposition to be fair in your dealing with others (Moral Strength). At the end of each day, write in the back of your journal about the following question:

Self: Was I fair in my dealings with others today? Answer the question in writing for a minimum of 2 minutes.

Others: (Business) Ask the following questions to your team: What does playing fair mean in our business? How can we be just in our dealings with others and still compete in the marketplace? Why should fairness matter to us as team members? Who cares if we cross the line of injustice? (Family) Ask family members to report any acts of justice or injustice that they have witnessed during the week. Have each person give one example of how he or she showed fairness in dealing with others during the week.

Rate Yourself:

1   2   3   4   5

Relatively Weak   Relatively Strong

CHARACTER CALL-OUTS

For You   For Work   For Family

HONOR

Definition: The acquired disposition to have one's actions and decisions reflect the highest ethical standards (Moral Strength).

Self: Honor, along with moral integrity, honesty, and justice represents the gold standards of moral character strength. To be a person of honor means you operate according to the highest ethical standards in your dealings with others. It represents a supreme character attainment. The character muscle of honor emerges from a crystal-clear set of values and beliefs that compel one to act in accordance with those ideals. Begin by formulating your grand purpose for living and then define the rules of engagement that naturally flow from that purpose.

Others: (Business) Discuss what it means to conduct oneself in an honorable way on the team. How do leaders display honor in their everyday activities, and how important is honor to team success? How might one undermine the team's honor? (Family) How might a family member dishonor himself or herself? How might a family member dishonor the family? To act according to one's highest ethical standards, one must know what those standards are. Ask each family member to prioritize their highest ethical principles and values.

Rate Yourself:

1	2	3	4	5
Relatively Weak				Relatively Strong

CHARACTER CALL-OUTS

For You   For Work   For Family

FORTITUDE

Definition: The acquired disposition to relentlessly fight for what's right (Performance Strength).

Self: The willingness and ability to fight for what we believe is right is foundational to a successful life. We fight by continuing to invest energy in a cause, and we surrender when we no longer are willing and able to invest our energy. Make a list of the things you are willing to fight for regardless of the cost. Grade yourself on the strength of your commitment to fight for those things you listed. Becoming a great fighter requires extraordinary, intentional investment of your best energy in the cause.

Others: (Business) Have each team member list the most sacred values and principles for the team that everyone must fight to uphold. Have team members grade themselves and the team as a whole, showing fortitude regarding their list. Discuss what fighting means and how it pertains to energy investment. (Family) Have each family member list all the things that are worth fighting for regardless of the effort required or cost. Discuss what "fighting for" means and how it relates to fortitude in life.

Rate Yourself:

1	**2**	**3**	**4**	**5**
Relatively Weak				Relatively Strong

CHARACTER CALL-OUTS

For You   For Work   For Family

TRUTHFULNESS

Definition: The acquired disposition to accurately report events and facts as you know them (Moral Strength).

Self: No one wants to think of himself or herself as untruthful or dishonest. It's simply too painful to acknowledge. Being truthful with others begins by being truthful with yourself, and confronting the truth about how reality-based your storytelling is to yourself and to others. Strengthening the truthfulness muscle begins by (1) openly confronting the deficiency, (2) setting a goal to strengthen it, and (3) keeping a daily written record of all your training investments. Hold yourself accountable for maintaining a high standard of truth to yourself and to others. Hold a very firm line.

Others: (Business) Discuss how truthfulness might be the single most important character strength in business success and effective leadership. Discuss how a culture of trust is built and maintained. Use examples from Stephen M. R. Covey's book *The Speed of Trust* for discussion. (Family) Discuss why truthfulness and honesty are so important to success in life. Explore the motivations people have for being dishonest. Why is it so hard for people to tell the truth? Have each family member bring one example of where telling the truth was difficult to do. Discuss the consequences for not being able to trust someone.

Rate Yourself:

1	2	3	4	5

Relatively Weak   Relatively Strong

CHARACTER CALL-OUTS

For You   For Work   For Family

AUTHENTICITY

Definition: The acquired disposition to align one's Public and Private Voice; to be genuine (Moral Strength).

Self: Set a daily goal to (1) more accurately align your inner and public voices and (2) align your inner and public voices with your deepest values. Your intent is to increase your sincerity quotient by aligning your Private and Public Voices with your core values.

Others: (Business) Discuss with team members what authenticity in leadership looks like and why it is important. Ask for concrete examples. Why do we distrust so many politicians? Why do so many politicians lose their authenticity? What's the lesson for leaders? (Family) Discuss what it means to be phony or insincere. How and why does it happen? What is the risk of telling people what they want to hear to keep them happy? What does it mean to be a genuine person, and how important is it for success in life? Give one example of being authentic in the last week that was difficult for you. How does one align his or her Public and Private Voice? What does that do?

Rate Yourself:

	1	2	3	4	5

Relatively Weak   Relatively Strong

CHARACTER CALL-OUTS

For You   For Work   For Family

WISDOM

Definition: The acquired disposition to formulate insights into the deeper meaning of life (Performance Strength).

Self: Spend time reading the works of the world's greatest thinkers from Plato and Aristotle to Viktor Frankl and the world's great spiritual teachers.

Others: (Business) Discuss in team meetings how wisdom is demonstrated in leadership. Discuss its relevance to leadership and how the capacity can be nurtured. (Family) Select two or three pages from thought-provoking books for all family members to read and discuss in the context of wisdom. Discuss characters in movies in the context of wisdom.

Rate Yourself:

1	**2**	**3**	**4**	**5**

Relatively Weak   Relatively Strong

CHARACTER CALL-OUTS

For You   For Work   For Family

ENGAGEMENT WITH OTHERS

Definition: The acquired disposition to bring your full and best energy to the present moment in your interactions with others (Moral Strength).

Self: Full engagement is the greatest gift we have to give to the world. Bringing our full and best energy in the present moment to our interactions with others honors their presence and is a gesture of deep respect. Full engagement is hard work and requires considerable energy-management skill. The ability to invest energy in the moment has physical, emotional, mental, and spiritual components. After every interpersonal interaction, rate yourself on the strength of your engagement. Was the quantity, quality, focus, and intensity of your energy the best you had to give? Hold yourself accountable for the investment of your energy in every interaction. The strength of your engagement muscle will steadily grow as you do so.

Others: (Business) Set the goal for team members to be fully engaged in meetings, fully engaged with clients, fully engaged with each other. Your intent is to establish a fully engaged culture. Frequently ask team members to rate their engagement levels in all their interactions at work. Quantification increases awareness, and awareness spawns growth. (Family) Begin by explaining what engagement is and why it is so important in life. This is also a great time to introduce the idea of managing their energy. Help each family member understand how important this character muscle is to success in life and even to personal happiness. Have family members pick five times each day to reflect on their level of engagement at that time for one week. Use a 1 to 5 scale where 1 is fully disengaged and 5 is fully engaged. Report back to the family with scores and what each was doing when the assessment was made. The mandate is simple: Engage when it's important and disengage when it's not.

Rate Yourself:

1	2	3	4	5
Relatively Weak				Relatively Strong

CHAPTER 3

Who Is the True Architect of Our Character?

It matters not how strait the gate,

How charged with punishments the scroll,

I am the master of my fate,

I am the captain of my soul.—William Ernest Henley, "Invictus"

How much do you "own" the formation of your character? Working to understand better the mechanics behind judging right from wrong can be a deeply rewarding personal journey. To own our character means that we built it, intentionally and consciously. It belongs to us. We were not given it, nor did we inherit it. We are not renting it or leasing it. We have constructed it based on life as we have come to experience it, on the people we have come to love and respect, on our most enduring and profound insights, on those beliefs and values that we've come to cherish and hold sacred. This source code for judging right from wrong, for determining True North on our moral compass, is what we mean by the term Personal Credo.

Whether or not we're aware of the origin of our moral code, we tap into it to determine what we do and don't do. It guides us in our treatment of others and in our efforts to live a moral life.

Which choice more accurately reflects your perception of the origin of your moral code?

1. I'm not certain of the origin of my core values and beliefs, and even less certain about how they were formed. My moral code just seemed to evolve naturally without much conscious intervention from me.

2. I take full ownership of the moral code I use in determining right from wrong. I own it because I have been actively building and maintaining it for years. It has been created, modified, and deployed with full intentionality.

From my years doing this work, I've learned that most leaders feel choice #1 is closer to their truth. The intent of this book is to change your answer to #2.

Following are 10 questions for you to reflect on. Write your answers in the accompanying Leading with Character journal, in a separate notebook, or on paper. Be as thoughtful and honest as possible, knowing that you can destroy and discard any of your writing that you would not want anyone else to see.

1. As you reflect on it now, who is the true author/owner of the moral code you use to determine right from wrong? Is it still your parents, your religious teachers, the culture you were brought up in, and so forth?

2. At what point in your life, if ever, did you consciously and intentionally create your own personal code of ethics? Put another way, when did you assume responsibility for the beliefs, values, and principles that guide your moral decisions and actions at work and at home?

3. If you are a deeply religious person, are your religious beliefs aligned with the moral character strengths presented in Chapter 1 – kindness, love, honesty, gratitude, generosity, patience, trustworthiness, and so forth? Where on the scale of importance is your moral character (e.g., your treatment of others, your respect for those who hold different belief(s)) in the hierarchy of your religious beliefs and values?

4. Have you ever seriously questioned or examined the moral beliefs, values, and traditions handed down to you from others? If so, did it lead you to change any of your beliefs and

values? Which beliefs and values, upon examination, have you kept or changed?

5. Are you aware of flaws in your process for determining what you should or shouldn't do morally (e.g., a propensity to use flawed logic; a "skill" to con yourself, guilt-free, into doing or getting what you really want; etc.). Explain.

6. When you make a moral decision, what do you call on to make the judgment? Explain.

7. Do you rely more on reason or emotions to "get it right" morally? How important are your gut feelings?

8. Does your heart or your head play the dominant role in your moral deliberations?

9. As you reflect on the big moral decisions you've made as a leader, which played a more dominant role: being tough-minded or being compassionate?

10. To what extent do you suspect your moral judgment is negatively influenced by hidden needs and wants that reside outside your ordinary awareness? Have you ever found yourself wondering, "Where did those questionable thoughts come from?" or "What made me say such a hurtful or cruel thing?"

Consider your most recent moral dilemma as a leader. Bring your deliberative process into the full light of consciousness by writing it out. Was your decision made quickly or slowly? Was it more feeling-based or fact-based? Were feelings and facts not so easily separated? Did you do what you determined to be the right thing? Did you let factors gain influence that could have – maybe should have – been set aside? In retrospect, did you make the right decision?

Beliefs that are not allowed to be questioned become relegated to the realm of superstition. Courage to question paves the way to truth.

THREE MINDS, TWO BRAINS, ONE BODY

We are complex creatures. I have come to understand that owning our moral character requires the integration of the entire spectrum of who we are as human beings.

Let's first explore the mind's involvement.

The existence of "mind" became reality when the forces of evolution made human consciousness possible. With the addition of a frontal cortex to our brains, we now possessed self-awareness, which enabled us to (among many other things) be aware of the process we use to judge right from wrong; of the emotions, beliefs, values, and logic that influence our choices. The story of humankind's spiritual evolution is directly linked to this ascension to higher awareness; the door to everything from self-directed personal change to spiritual enlightenment was opened. Conscious awareness and morality are inexorably bound together; morality does not exist without the capacity for consciousness. Higher morality becomes accessible only in the expansion and deepening of personal awareness. That's precisely why I had you consider the previous 10 questions.

Unfortunately, at any given moment, only a fraction of what our brain perceives resides in the realm of the conscious. By "conscious," I mean the content that is fully available in our moment-to-moment awareness. To raise the moral awareness of leaders to the highest possible level, it is imperative to bring one's moral reasoning and judgment process into the full light of consciousness. This will stop leaders from ever again defaulting to quick, reflexive, gut-driven moral decisions that can have disastrous consequences. When leaders are asked to recall moral decisions they now regret, it's common to hear, "I really never thought the consequences through" or "It was almost like someone else made the decision, not me." When leaders abdicate responsibility and ownership for their poor moral decisions by suggesting that the actions weren't really like them, that it was out of character for them, it is simply an attempt to reduce their culpability from their perspective. A well-constructed, intentionally designed morality system combined with full consciousness resolves such issues.

LEVELS OF CONSCIOUSNESS

There is the *conscious mind* (Mind 1), where moment-to-moment awareness rules. Just below the surface of awareness resides the *subconscious mind* (Mind 2). In most cases, contents of the subconscious mind can be made conscious by intentionally calling the contents forward – for instance, remembering what your father said to you when he learned you cheated on an exam in school. Below the subconscious mind resides the vast and more mysterious *unconscious mind* (Mind 3); its contents are generally beyond conscious reach. Instinctive urges, hidden desires, unresolved conflicts, early childhood traumas, fears of all kinds – these and so much more occupy the space of the unconscious. Because much of the contents of the unconscious are perceived to be too disruptive to our normal functioning, we deploy – unconsciously! – a variety of defensive measures to keep the information from breaking into consciousness.

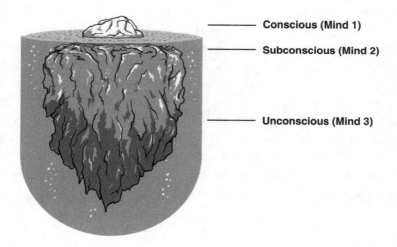

    Conscious (Mind 1)

    Subconscious (Mind 2)

    Unconscious (Mind 3)

The iceberg analogy is often used to depict human consciousness. The area above the waterline is the conscious mind. Just below the waterline is the subconscious mind; below that, in the darker reaches, resides the massive realm of the unconscious. Here's another analogy I like: In the space of the conscious mind, all the lights are on; in the subconscious space, lights are selectively turned on; in the unconscious space, all lights are off. Or, to use psychologist Jonathan Haidt's metaphor of the rider and the elephant: The tiny rider attempting to control the elephant is the conscious mind; the massive elephant represents the subconscious and unconscious mind. The more the rider is aware of the elephant's needs, stress, rhythms, tendencies, habits, and so forth, the more success he or she will have in exercising control. Similarly, for leaders to own and control their moral lives, awareness must be enabled whenever and wherever possible.

When your moral choices and actions are illuminated with the full light of conscious awareness, the odds of living your Best Moral Self turns decidedly in your favor.

Two Brains

The first of our two brains has been around for thousands of years. This old guy, our "emotional brain," consists of structures like the brain stem and cerebellum. The brain stem regulates bodily functions like breathing, heartbeat, and body temperature. Resting atop the brain stem is a structure called the diencephalon, which controls sleep and hunger cycles. Moving higher up the brain resides the limbic system, which is comprised of structures like the amygdala, hippocampus, and hypothalamus. Although the hypothalamus represents less than 1% of the brain's mass, it controls most endocrine functions plus many aspects of emotion. It is in this limbic architecture that the feelings and emotions of the brain are generated.

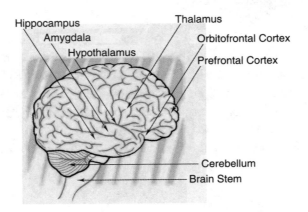

The second of the two brains, the "rational brain" or cortex, represent the new kid on the block. It rests just above the limbic system. With this "new" neuroprocessing system, we are now able to think abstractly and analyze logically. It was not until this second brain developed that humans were capable of complex language.

For centuries, long before advances in neuroscience shed light on the issue, philosophers elevated our capacity for reason to the highest possible status. The ancient Greeks perceived humankind's most noble side to be the rational side. Plato equated emotions with animal passions, and reason with moral goodness and wisdom. Many centuries later, Descartes divided our essence into two categories: a sacred soul, from which thought and reason flowed, and a physical body that produced "mechanical passions." The prevailing wisdom for centuries was that our rational brain opened the door to moral goodness, while our emotional brain suppressed it.

Ownership of our morality requires openness to messages being sent from both our rational and emotional brains.

Advances in neuroscience have turned this thinking on its head. Our emotional brains and rational brains are not and should not be disconnected entities. Researchers have shown that a significant part of our frontal cortex is involved with emotion. According to neuroscientist Antonio Damasio, feelings are an integral component of the machinery of reason. Damasio identified a small neurological circuit, called the orbitofrontal cortex (OFC), as critical to linking our emotional and rational brains. Our emotional brain represents, in fact, a remarkable resource of moral wisdom and intelligence, thanks to thousands of years of evolutionary learning. When an accident or trauma severs the links between our emotional and rational brains, our capacity for sound moral reasoning and judgment is impaired. Neuroscientist Joseph LeDoux contends that much of what we think from our rational brain is driven by messages from our emotional brain.

Ownership of our morality requires openness to messages being sent from both our rational and emotional brains. Just as rational thinking and logical analysis are crucial components in the formation of our morality, so are feelings like compassion, kindness, and empathy. Human morality simply cannot prevail without consciousness – and neither can it prevail without the integration of reason and emotion. When we disparage the value of our emotions, when we limit our morality to rational thinking only, owning our morality is simply not possible, because an important voice inside us has been shut down.

MORAL JUDGMENT AND OXYTOCIN

In 2011, Simon Baron-Cohen, professor of developmental psychopathology at the University of Cambridge, published *The Science of Evil*, which argued that evil is the consequence of blocked empathy and compassion. Without empathy, Baron-Cohen contended, we can turn people into objects, and all that's left is "I." He defined empathy as the ability to identify what someone else is thinking or feeling and to respond appropriately. For Baron-Cohen, empathy is the most valuable moral resource in the world; it represents a universal solvent for evil.

Neuroscientists have discerned at least 10 regions of the brain are involved in what Baron-Cohen calls "the empathy circuit"; one of these is the (previously mentioned) OFC, which helps link our rational and emotional brains. Empathy is both a cognitive understanding and an emotional response.

Neuroscientist Kent Kiehl, after scanning the brains of more than 4,000 prison inmates, found structural impairment in areas connecting thoughts and emotions, most notably in the OFC. According to Kiehl, psychopaths think about what's right and wrong but cannot feel it. Healthy moral reasoning incorporates both thinking and feeling; tragically, the moral machinery of psychopaths restricts this critical integration.

The emotions that play a central role in an individual's healthy moral calculus – and that are blocked in an unhealthy one – include kindness, compassion, caring, and trust, all of which possess the same neuropeptide oxytocin. Oxytocin consists of nine amino acids and is primarily produced in the nuclei of the hypothalamus. Sometimes referred to as the "love hormone," early research on oxytocin focused on the hormone's ability to strengthen the bond between mother and child. Oxytocin plasma concentrations rise dramatically during the birthing process. As oxytocin levels increase, social distance closes. Feelings of trust, compassion, empathy, and caring increase.

The empathy circuit, as well as related feelings of kindness, compassion, caring, and trust, not only share a common biochemical substrate (oxytocin) but, more importantly, represent an indispensable source of input in our process of moral deliberation. As with muscles in the physical body, when the "muscles" of empathy, compassion, and caring are strengthened through training, they become more available to us in our efforts to say or do the right thing. Owning our moral code requires that we decide where, in our hierarchy of values, empathy, compassion, kindness, and the like fall compared with values such as being a winner, succeeding in competition, and ambition. Owning our moral code is impossible unless we, as leaders, prioritize values that dictate how we treat and interact with others.

There's something inherently threatening about questioning the ownership and legitimacy of one's moral code. Part of that may be a fear of disrespecting our parents, grandparents, religious teachers, and so forth. Perhaps we're afraid of what we might find in the searching. Maybe we fear that our identity as a moral person could be destabilized as we probe for answers. Regardless, it's imperative that we push past doubts and fears, and bring our moral code into full awareness. When we confront the truth about ownership, about how responsible we feel for the beliefs and values that form the bedrock of our sense of right and wrong, we move inexorably toward living an authentic life. As one client put it, "Now I realize I've been living in a moral fog most of my life. The fog has been steadily lifting since I started asking tough questions and making daily entries into my journal. My moral awareness has significantly improved. I can't say my moral deliberation process is any easier, but I can say I have much greater confidence in whatever moral actions I take because of it."

CHARACTER CALL-OUTS

For You   For Work   For Family

CRITICAL THINKING

Definition: The acquired disposition to think in a reality-based way (Performance Strength).

Self: Set a goal to improve your critical thinking skills by making a list of pros and cons for every major decision you're trying to make. After putting the facts down on paper and carefully reviewing them, what does logic tell you? Your objective is to sharpen your logical thinking skills.

Others: (Business) Present a current problem facing the team that requires a decision. Get all the facts on the table and ask everyone to use logic and reality-based thinking to explore a solution. Compare results and discuss the logic. (Family) Use real-life problems facing the family or family members that require a decision be made to sharpen critical thinking skills. Get all the critical facts on the table and encourage everyone to be logical and reality-based in their thinking. Compare results from each family member.

Rate Yourself:

| 1 | 2 | 3 | 4 | 5 |

Relatively Weak   Relatively Strong

CHARACTER CALL-OUTS

For You   For Work   For Family

PRUDENCE

Definition: The acquired disposition to exercise good judgment (Performance Strength).

Self: Exercising good judgment requires touching three important sources of wisdom. The first is, "What are the facts?" Second, "What does your heart say?" and third, "What does your gut say?" When making important decisions, consciously touch all these bases of wisdom before executing. Keep a record of the decisions you make using this reflective process.

Others: (Business) Prudent decision-making is a critical component of effective leadership. Help team members understand that prudent decision-making is an acquired skill that must be constantly trained and conditioned. Ask team members for examples of decision-making where all three sources of wisdom were considered before a decision was made. Place a high value on prudent decision-making in the culture. (Family) Explain to family members what prudent decision-making means and requires. Provide the three-step process for them to follow. Ask family members to give one example each week of a decision they make that met all the requirements for prudence.

Rate Yourself:

1	**2**	**3**	**4**	**5**
Relatively Weak				Relatively Strong

CHARACTER CALL-OUTS

For You   For Work   For Family

DISCERNMENT

Definition: The acquired disposition to seek the deeper causes for things (Performance Strength).

Self: Discernment helps us to make thoughtful, intelligent choices in life and avoid reactive, foolish ones. It's the ability to look beyond surface observations and explore the deeper implications and consequences for the choices we make. Write a list of the long- and short-term consequences that are likely to follow from making a particular decision. Pick two or three decisions to discern each week and prepare your consequences list prior to making your decision.

Others: (Business) To build discernment in team members, take one decision facing the team each week and have team members look beyond surface observations by listing possible unintended consequences that need to be considered before making the final decision. (Family) Set the goal to improve every family member's ability to make good choices by strengthening their discernment muscle. Spend 5 to 10 minutes each week exploring the pros and cons of making a particular decision for an issue facing the family. Special attention should be given to hidden, unintended possible consequences. Once the issues have been fully explored, have the family make a decisive decision.

Rate Yourself:

1   2   3   4   5

Relatively Weak   Relatively Strong

CHARACTER CALL-OUTS

For You   For Work   For Family

DECISIVENESS

Definition: The acquired disposition to make definitive choices (Performance Strength).

Self: Give yourself specific time limits on everyday decisions such as ordering from menus, selecting a movie, buying shoes or clothes, deciding what to do or where to go on your day off. Once you make your decision, live with it. No last-second changes. By living with the consequences, your decision process will get sharper, more effective, and more focused.

Others: (Business) Discuss the importance of decisiveness in effective leadership. Give examples of being decisive and not decisive in work decisions. What are the consequences of indecisiveness for team members? (Family) Have a family discussion on how good decisions are made and why it's important to be decisive. What's the problem with always changing your mind, constantly putting off decisions, and always regretting the decisions you make? Practice making good, decisive decisions over the next three weeks and report back to the family with concrete examples.

Rate Yourself:

1   **2**   **3**   **4**   **5**

Relatively Weak   Relatively Strong

CHARACTER CALL-OUTS

For You   For Work   For Family

CONFIDENCE

Definition: The acquired disposition to believe in one's abilities (Performance Strength).

Self: A major component of confidence in oneself is the tone and content of one's Private Voice. One's Inner Voice is critical in building a solid base of confidence. Commit to building your confidence muscle by repeatedly writing about how you want to speak to yourself going forward. Think of what you would say to your best friend to help build his or her confidence. Build confidence by focusing your efforts on things under your control – attitude, effort, mistake management, body language, and so forth.

Others: (Business) Discuss the importance of confidence to team success. Explore the following questions: (1) How do great coaches build confidence? (2) How important is one's Private Voice in building stable confidence? (3) What scorecard should team members use to define success and build confidence? (Family) Parents should reward effort over outcome every time. Make sure your child does not use winning and losing as the basis for building his or her confidence or self-esteem. Confidence should always be connected to things under their direct control. Have several family discussions on the importance of confidence in life and how best to build it.

Rate Yourself:

1	2	3	4	5

Relatively Weak   Relatively Strong

Character Call-Outs

For You   For Work   For Family

COMPETITIVENESS

Definition: The acquired disposition to enjoy pitting your skills against the skills of others (Performance Strength).

Self: Individuals who fear competition with others are at a severe disadvantage in today's world. Start competing in areas that are inconsequential in terms of threat. Examples might be who can do the most situps in a minute, who can balance on one foot the longest or who can pick the closest score in tonight's pro basketball game. Eventually, raise the consequences for winning or losing the competition by betting money, privileges, or favors. Commit to a minimum of two competitions per week for four weeks and keep a detailed record.

Others: (Business) Create a variety of inter-team and intra-team competitions to build competitive strength and spawn team spirit. From sales numbers to fitness challenges, the opportunities for strengthening the competitive muscle are nearly limitless. (Family) Card games, spelling bees, sports predictions, school grades, and so forth can be used to build competitive skills of family members.

Rate Yourself:

1	2	3	4	5
Relatively Weak				Relatively Strong

CHARACTER CALL-OUTS

For You   For Work   For Family

AMBITION

Definition: The acquired disposition to be goal-oriented and goal-directed (Performance Strength).

Self: Understanding the connection between goal-setting and achievement is an important insight in life. Goal-setting establishes a target for your energy investments. The character muscle of ambition can be strengthened by repeatedly setting goals, investing in the accomplishment of those goals, and in achieving them.

Others: (Business) Goal-setting is as crucial to success in business as it is in sport. The ability to be ambitious and find satisfaction in achievement can be strengthened through successful goal-setting. Both team and individual goals should be established within the team structure. Goals can be short-term, intermediate, or long-term. Every team member should understand that one of the purposes for goal-setting is to strengthen the achieving/ambition character disposition. (Family) As with most all character strengths, the family is the most important place to begin the strengthening process. Setting goals for school grades, sports achievements, saving money, fitness, and so forth builds the foundation for this character strength. Goals can be process-based or outcome-based. Spending a minimum of 20 minutes each day on homework is process-based, and achieving a 3.0 grade point average is outcome-based.

Rate Yourself:

1	2	3	4	5
Relatively Weak				Relatively Strong

CHAPTER 4

Who Are We Becoming in the Chase to the Top?

This is the true joy in life, the being used for a purpose recognized by yourself as a mighty one; the being thoroughly worn out before you are thrown on the scrap heap; the being a force of nature instead of a feverish selfish little clod of ailments and grievances complaining that the world will not devote itself to making you happy.—George Bernard Shaw

Since our first appearance on Earth, we have been chasing. Chasing food, survival, comfort, love, sex, security, happiness, fulfillment. Chasing fame, money, social status, power, privilege, titles, beauty, and on and on. We love to chase, to be all in, to be fully energized in the pursuit of something. Chasing is apparently in our DNA.

In your quest to lead with character, consider these questions:

1. What am I chasing?

2. Why am I chasing it?

3. Who am I becoming as a consequence of the chase? Who are those that I lead becoming?

What are you chasing? Why are you chasing it? Who are you and all those you are leading becoming as a consequence of the chase?

We chase things that we see value in owning, possessing, achieving. Thousands of years ago, Aristotle asked, "What is the ultimate purpose of human society?" Before that, Socrates had proclaimed, "The unexamined life is not worth living." This shows just how far back humankind has been searching for answers to the provocative questions of who we really are and why we're here. (And the search precedes the ancient Greeks.)

WHERE SHOULD WE LOOK FOR ANSWERS?

In philosophy and psychology, much attention has been given to the notion of the "true self" – that therein lies the source code for answering life's most challenging questions. In classic psychological theory, the true self is conceived as a set of innate, immutable characteristics that must be discovered to achieve a truly fulfilling, meaningful life. To unearth our true self and behave in accordance with it is to achieve life satisfaction, happiness, and well-being. Aligning our lives with the true self, according to this theory, connects us to our essence and becomes the basis for living an authentic life.

As a graduate student in psychology, I struggled with the concept of the true self. The notion that I just needed to keep searching and eventually I would uncover who I really was: That never resonated with me. Research about the true self construct was sketchy, at best. But even more troubling for me, personally, was the idea that the blueprint for who I was to become was pre-determined and innate.

There is a contemporary alternative to the notion of the pre-determined, immutable true self, an alternative more aligned with our experiences and practices at the Institute. It's called Self-Determination Theory (SDT). According to this theory, who we are to become is not something that's innately acquired, but internally self-determined. That is, *Our fate resides not in the discovery of what lies within us, but in the active process of creating it.*

From our decades of work at the Institute, answers to the questions of what we are to chase, why we are to chase it, and who we are to become in the process are not found in the discovery of our true self. They are created actively and intentionally.

FROM TRUE SELF TO BEST SELF

An alternative to looking for one's true self is looking for one's "best self." According to our clients, this search produces a trove of insights. Here's how it works:

Take a few minutes and reflect on when you are most proud of yourself; on when you are the very best you can be as a person. This is not a fantasy "wish I could be" exercise. It is about you assessing when you are the best you can be in the real world. After all, we all become the best version of ourselves from time to time. Maybe it doesn't happen nearly as often as we would like; but it surely happens at times. Reflecting on when these moments happen is precisely what you're focusing on for this exercise.

It's sometimes helpful to think of the best you have to offer physically, emotionally, mentally, and spiritually. Reflect on when your best self emerged in stressful or challenging situations. Now, considering when you are most proud of yourself, write down six one-word descriptors that best capture who you really are in these moments.

1. _____

2. _____

3. _____

4. _____

5. _____

6. _____

We've done this simple exercise with thousands of participants. When asked to share their choices with the group, nearly everyone is shocked to learn how similar, even identical, their word choices are to others in the class. The most common descriptors are words like "caring," "kind," "patient," "compassionate," "grateful," and "authentic." Less common are words like "happy," "focused," "satisfied," peaceful," and "positive." Noticeably absent are words like "ambitious," "achieving," "successful," "driven," and "winning." With no prodding, the majority of respondents selected words that connected them to others. As one participant put it, "It seems like we all copied from each other."

A related exercise that yields equally surprising results: Participants are asked to list the six words that best describe how they most want to be remembered after their death.

Make your list:

1. _____

2. _____

3. _____

4. _____

5. _____

6. _____

Again, when participants read their lists aloud, almost everyone in the class is amazed. The same words used to capture who they were at their best were also used to describe how they wanted to be remembered. Words like "integrity," "generous," "loving," "humble," "empathetic," and "engaged" kept appearing on both lists. After this pattern repeated itself time and again, year after year, it was clear that for most participants the reference point for who they are at their best and how they want to be remembered in life was, simply put, their moral character. The most important measure for creating both lists was how virtuous they were in their treatment of others.

These two reflective exercises accomplish several goals.

1. They remind us how important moral character is to true success in life.

2. They bring us face to face with the core values that represent the building blocks of our Personal Credo.

3. They help us to answer the "chasing questions" asked at the beginning of this chapter.

ULTIMATE MEASURE:
Our Treatment of Others

The reference point for who we are at our best and how we want to be remembered after we are gone is our treatment of others.

CHOOSE YOUR PURPOSE CAREFULLY

Chasing the wrong thing, and chasing the right thing for the wrong reason, can have tragic consequences. Too many of us have been duped into believing that great achievements represent the essential material of a truly successful life. In my previous book, *The Only Way to Win*, I examined the fake belief that great achievements are the key to lasting happiness, stable self-esteem, strong moral character, and enduring success in life. Despite the fact that no research evidence exists for such a belief, people continue to pursue achievement feverishly, certain that it will. In his book *Life on Purpose*, researcher Vic Strecher, who went through our training in 2009 and went on to write books and create a company focused on purpose in 2014, issued a stern warning: "A bad purpose can go horribly wrong. Handle with care!" From our decades of work at the Institute, I can say he is absolutely right. The most important work we do with our clients, unquestionably, is helping them to connect to their deepest values and to a *truly meaningful purpose*. Once these are in place, answering the chasing questions follows quite naturally. When we get the "why" right, everything we do as leaders changes. When our ultimate "why" is the well-being of those we lead or those our company serves, a seismic shift occurs in everything we do and say. When we put the needs of others ahead of our own, when we display caring, compassion, and respect for others instead of indulging ourselves, when issues of justice, fairness, integrity, and kindness outrank personal ambition, wealth, and social status, it nourishes not only those we lead but also whatever business we are in. According to researchers Raj Sisodia, David Wolfe, and Jag Sheth, when leadership endears itself to the functional and psychological needs of those they lead, the business results are often extraordinary. According to their research, such companies, referred to as "Firms of Endearment," returned 1,026% for investors over the 10 years ending June 30, 2006, compared to 122% for the S&P 500 over the same time period – better than an 8 to 1 ratio. In a business where purpose is too often defined narrowly, including only maximizing profits and shareholder value, words like "compassion," "caring," "empathy," and "love" would seem to have no real place. Yet evidence mounts that companies that expanded their purpose to include improving the well-being of those that work for them – termed "Deliberately Developmental Organizations" by Harvard researchers Lisa Lahey and Robert Kegan – create a win/win proposition, a win both for shareholders and employees. When employees feel cared for as human beings, apart from the contributions they make to the company's bottom line, they are more likely to care about their employer. When a leader fully embraces a purpose that includes taking care of his or her people, when the "how we do it" of a business is given priority equal to or greater than the "what we do," we see positive trends in talent attraction and retention, employee engagement, and profitability. More importantly, a leader's concern for the welfare of those he or she leads needs no longer to be checked at the firm's front door. Your core purpose as a leader and the core purpose of the company are in full alignment.

Would you be as excited to help others if no one knew the help came from you?

Three additional chase-related issues are relevant here.

Can human beings find real fulfillment and well-being without knowing the "why," or purpose, behind what they are chasing?

Can we find sustained happiness when our reason for chasing is feeling good ourselves – that is, maximizing our own pleasure and minimizing our own pain? Put another way: Can a hedonistic life ever truly be a fulfilling life? (It's a question that's been considered for thousands of years, beginning with the Greek philosophers Epicurus and Aristippus.)

Our humanity is manifested most brilliantly in our treatment of others.

Is life more likely to be fulfilling when the purpose of our chasing is more about others than ourselves? Put another way: How important is it to shift from a self-enhancing purpose to a self-transcending one?

At our Institute, we've pursued answers to such purpose-centered questions for nearly three decades. And our answers are more or less aligned with Aristotle, Seligman, Emmons, Frankl, Deci, Ryan, Gardner, and so many other scholars and researchers. From the considerable evidence we've gathered, we believe firmly that who we are to become is not to be found like a prize in a treasure hunt. Our life purpose, our values, our choices, and our moral character are ultimately self-determined. It is through our remarkable capacity for conscious awareness and personal reflection that the active process of self-determination is made possible. Our humanness manifests most brilliantly in our treatment of others – all others. Strengths of integrity, honesty, caring, authenticity, compassion, empathy, justice, and humility define not only how we are to fulfill our self-determined purpose but how we want to be remembered after we are gone. Human beings are clearly purpose-driven. And our most powerful, sustaining sense of purpose occurs when we transcend self-interest and extend our reach to a concern for others, when the *why* behind what we do is intrinsic and other-centered.

What *appears* to be ironic, then, is that we get a life by giving it away. We become happy by making others happy. As the Dalai Lama expressed so eloquently, "If you want others to be happy, practice compassion; if you want to be happy, practice compassion."

What we chase in life is far less important than our reason for chasing it.

What we chase in life is far less important than our reason for chasing it. When our why is improving the well-being of others, we can leverage value from most any activity or job, provided it does not harm others in the process. As to the questions, Who are we becoming? and Who are those we lead becoming as a consequence of the chase? The answer to both is simple: We become stronger in all aspects of moral character. Which is good for us and good for those we lead.

WHERE PURPOSE CAN FALL SHORT

While purpose is a key component for helping individuals find meaning in their work and lives, there is a need to go beyond identifying and declaring purpose as a means to achieve individual and organizational well-being.

It is important to note that personal and organizational purpose are NOT the same. Leaders often become solely focused on organizational purpose – the purpose and mission of the company they lead. This can be out of a sense of duty or simply from a lack of reflection on the difference between their own purpose and the mission of the company. This lack of differentiation is especially observed in "helping" organizations such as NGOs or healthcare companies that are dedicated to improving or saving lives. For those leaders who might argue that they must be fully invested in their company's purpose, an effective response is to ask, "If you are removed from your role tomorrow, does your purpose in life disappear?" When leaders do not prioritize their personal purpose, well-being, and life, the results can be devastating as they sacrifice their own health, family, and relationships, as well as their ability to effectively lead their teams and consistently make sound and ethical decisions.

CAN OUR CHARACTER MUSCLES BECOME TOO STRONG FOR THE CHASE?

Can you become *too* compassionate? Can a leader have *too* much empathy? Can the character muscles of the heart, like kindness and caring, become so strong that you can't make necessary decisions that will be discomforting or difficult for those you lead? Can you get so lost in being empathetic that you lose touch with objective reality, and with it your ability to lead effectively? Can you become so generous that you give everything away, too trusting that you constantly get duped, too humble that feelings of insecurity persist?

If the muscles of character are analogous to the physical muscles of the body, let's look there for insight. Can one's biceps, triceps, hamstrings, or quadriceps become too strong? Is strength ever dysfunctional in the physical body? A tennis player possessing the bicep strength of a world-champion weightlifter, or a figure skater with the quadricep strength of a football lineman, would likely be dysfunctional. A nurse or hospice worker probably needs stronger compassion and empathy muscles than an assembly line autoworker. Isn't it possible, however, that nurses can become so compassionate and empathetic toward their patients that they are unable to fulfill some of their basic duties? Can soldiers in battle be so consumed by empathy or compassion that they cannot complete their mission?

Let's consider three things.

First: Just as you do with a physical muscle, if you wish to strengthen a Character Muscle, feed it your energy until it grows to the capacity you desire. If you want its capacity to shrink, feed it less. You can intentionally invest energy in a Character Muscle by thinking about it, visualizing it, talking about it, acting it out, writing about it – and, of course, employing it. For example, if you want to grow your Compassion Muscle, you can think about why being compassionate is important to you. You can visualize yourself feeling compassion in situations that have previously given you trouble, such as always wanting to lift people up emotionally rather than "simply" listening to them and feeling their suffering. You can act out compassion in real-life situations and write about compassion in your daily journal. You can practice compassion meditation. Such intentional energy investments allow you to determine what you want your moral character to be and then create it. Morality requires all Character Muscles to be routinely conditioned, most importantly those governing how we interact with and treat others.

Second: The size of the muscle – its capacity – must be proportionate to the demands that will be placed on it. For example, the demand for bicep strength is considerably less for a golfer than for a power lifter.

Third: Muscle strengths must be in balance. Bicep strength must be balanced by tricep strength – or dysfunction is likely when extending or flexing the arm. A strong bicep and a weak tricep, or a strong hamstring and a weak quadricep, breed dysfunctionality. Major muscles like these are called "prime movers": They do the heavy lifting. The two counterbalancing muscular forces are called "agonist" and "antagonist." The agonist represents the main action of the muscle; the antagonist works opposite to the main muscle. In a bicep curl, the bicep is the agonist and the tricep is the antagonist. When the arm is extended, the tricep becomes the agonist, the bicep the antagonist. For the body to move effectively, all antagonistic muscle groups must be appropriately balanced.

For arm or leg muscles to move properly, some muscles must turn on and some must turn off at the same time. For example, in a bicep curl, the bicep contracts while the tricep simultaneously relaxes. This is called "reciprocal inhibition." Overactive or underactive muscles can cause muscle imbalance, dysfunction, and potentially pain and injury. The movement of the graceful athlete requires the synergistic switching on and off of all the muscles involved. Synergistic activation and deactivation make sure your muscular response is appropriate to the demands of the movement.

When you expect others to view you as an elite, you unknowingly reveal your character deficit in humility.

By this point you're probably wondering why I'm going through this detailed discourse on muscle physiology. Why?

Because everything I just wrote about the muscles of the physical body applies to the muscles of character.

Issues of muscle balance, muscle size, synergy, reciprocal inhibition, and the concepts of agonist and antagonist apply to both worlds. To give an example, the counterbalancing force to the agonist muscle of humility is confidence (the antagonist). Humility without confidence breeds insecurity. Likewise, the muscle of confidence without humility breeds arrogance. The muscle of authenticity can become dysfunctional without the counterbalancing muscles of kindness, compassion, caring, and so forth. Authenticity without counterbalance can give one license to say things that harm others under the guise of being, well, authentic. "I just have to be who I really am." When the muscles of the heart are not properly counterbalanced, you get "enlarged heart" or "bleeding heart." The counterbalancing muscles to prevent this could be the muscles of justice, tough-mindedness, or courage – perhaps referred to as "tough love." It's important to note that our character muscles can be strategically balanced with either oppositional *moral* muscles or oppositional *performance* muscles. This underscores why *all* Character Muscles, both moral and performance, need to be constantly stimulated, strengthened, and trained.

Let's explore an example more deeply.

The agonist character muscle of loyalty can become tragically dysfunctional without a counterbalancing muscle. Loyalty to the Mob, to a political party, to a sketchy business associate without balancing muscles such as justice or fairness could have disastrous consequences. Loyalty without counterbalance is really what we mean when we say "blind loyalty." Blind loyalty to a politician's party over loyalty to the people who elected him or her represents a form of moral failure.

Another example: When the moral muscle of generosity is unchecked by prudence, problems arise. The following illustration depicts the balancing/counterbalancing relationship.

Balancing Character Muscles

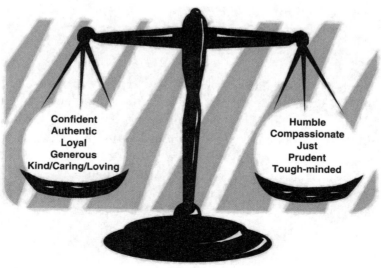

In the August 2017 issue of the *Harvard Business Review*, Tomas Chamorro-Premuzic and Derek Lusk issue a warning: "Too much muscle mass in the competency of resilience can be a bad thing." Extreme resilience, they argue, may result in people persisting with unrealistic, unattainable goals.

How do we at the Institute handle this? Not by encouraging a reduction in the robust muscles of resilience, persistence, grit, or determination, but rather by building the counterbalancing muscles of discernment, prudence, and critical thinking.

BALANCING HONESTY AND CARING

As reported in the *Journal of Experimental Social Psychology*, researchers Emma Levine and Maurice Schweitzer found that individuals who lied for benevolent reasons were perceived to be more ethical than those who simply told the truth; that is, when telling a falsehood was done intentionally to benefit others, the deception was judged to be more ethical than simply reporting the unvarnished truth. The findings of this study suggest that, for many, caring for others represents a higher moral value than honesty. Lying for self-serving purposes – cheating on exams, falsifying tax returns and résumés – is perceived to be a violation of character. The calculus changes, however, when the welfare of others is concerned. Levine and Schweitzer's research challenges the presumption that all deception is immoral, all honesty moral. Their finding underscores the nuances of morality. The notion of altruistic, pro-social lies versus harming others with pure honesty points, once again, to the importance of balance. Is it morally okay for doctors to present their prognosis in a more favorable light than warranted? Are those doctors being more moral or less by doing so? Can it ever be morally right to lie to your spouse – for example, to deny a brief affair that's now ended – because it would likely lead to divorce, great suffering for the children, and, when all is tallied, relatively more pain for your spouse? Are "white" lies – those meant to deceive but also to spare the recipient guaranteed anguish – ever morally justified? Answering such questions in a morally responsible, honorable way is why the deliberate, intentional construction of a Personal Credo is so important – and so challenging. Many such issues may be resolved only after deep personal reflection and examination of all the circumstances. So much moral wisdom grows out of the notion of balance.

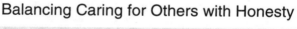

Balancing Caring for Others with Honesty

So: How do you balance caring for others with pure honesty?

AN AGONIST/ANTAGONIST RELATIONSHIP FROM THE WORLD OF POLITICS

At the core of American politics is a constant tension between opposing forces. An objective of American governance is balance – between the agonist of freedom (the prime mover) and the antagonist of fairness. Within the two dominant players, the Republican and Democratic parties, reside a multitude of agonist and antagonist forces. In broad terms, the prime muscle for Republicans is freedom, which moves them toward personal responsibility, personal initiative, and self-determination. Laws exist essentially to protect personal freedoms. Because laws tend to restrict personal freedoms, the fewer the better. The American Constitution represents the ultimate source code for governance.

Scale of Balance in Politics

The prime mover for Democrats is fairness, which motivates them toward just treatment for all, equal opportunities and privileges for all, and equal protections for all. Laws exist to ensure equal/fair treatment for every American, regardless of social status, race, or other identifiers that have historically engendered unfair/unequal treatment. As many laws as are necessary to protect people and the environment must be enacted. The source code for Democrats is not necessarily a document created 200+ years ago, but rather what is deemed right and just for today's world.

Can we feel the tension between the two opposing forces? Yes! Massively, and every day. As confidence devoid of humility leads to dysfunctional arrogance, so, too, freedom devoid of fairness or fairness devoid of freedom leads to a deeply dysfunctional state. Unbalanced freedom at the extreme becomes anarchy and utter chaos – the complete absence of government and protections – and, of course, doesn't feel like true freedom at all. Unbalanced fairness at the extreme becomes communism, even dictatorship – with government oppressively deter- mining everything – and, of course, doesn't feel like true fairness at all. Losing freedom or losing fairness each has catastrophic consequences. Both forces are necessary for effective governance. When balance hap- pens, we get capitalism with a heart, democracy with an engine for growth. History has shown repeatedly that America's best legislation occurs when the forces (input) from both parties are factored into the solution. Political gridlock means the agonist and antagonist relation- ship ceases to exist.

Similarly, in the case of moral reasoning and judgment, when our character strengths are not appropriately balanced with relevant counterbalancing strengths, any rendered judgment is likely to be flawed.

One of the greatest failures of leadership is "kicking the can down the road." Not having the courage to deal with the pain now — letting future leaders deal with it.

BALANCING POWER WITH COMPASSION

The nineteenth-century British historian Lord Acton famously proclaimed, "Absolute power corrupts absolutely." Historians point to the long, ugly litany of world leaders succumbing to the dark side once total power was placed in their hands. The world of business is replete with examples of great power spawning great corruption, greed, and exploitation.

Psychological researchers have linked those possessing power with an increased tendency to be rude, behave sexually inappropriately, flout the law, ignore the safety of others, share less, empathize less, listen less, act hypocritically, act dishonestly, and take what they want because they feel entitled to do so. Not a pretty picture.

According to Pamela Smith, researcher at the University of California, San Diego, those who have more self-centered values tend to be more selfish as they gain more power. Or, as Lincoln said, "Nearly all men can stand adversity, but if you want to test a man's character, give him power."

As you pursue the goal of leading with character, what can you do to mitigate risks that come with the power, whether you're a manager, senior manager, or C-suite executive? What moral muscles must be built to help leaders transcend the temptations to abuse their power?

Scale of Balance for Power

Researcher Katherine DeCelles at the University of Toronto provides insight into the question. DeCelles observed that power actually seemed to bring out the best in some people – so she explored the matter further, and her results and those of her colleagues were published in the *Journal of Applied Psychology*. Those whose self-identity was closely linked to compassion, caring, and fairness were likelier to use their power in more ethical ways. A predisposition to caring and compassion versus a predisposition to selfishness profoundly altered the power dynamic. The takeaway? When leaders are relentless in strengthening their moral muscles, particularly those of caring and compassion, they can and will resist the ever-present temptation to abuse power and privilege for selfish reasons.

TURNING MORAL MUSCLES ON AND OFF

There's a time to be compassionate and a time to be tough-minded. There's a time to display empathy and a time to display justice. There's also a time when being honest and authentic requires simultaneous compassion to get it morally right. Moral intelligence – doing the right thing at the right time – is acquired much in the same way a gymnast learns to execute a complex mount on the balance beam. In the latter case, the graceful patterns of precision movement result from the synergistic switching on and off of targeted motor-neuro connections, an extraordinary ballet of coordinated agonist and antagonist activity. The synchronized movement skills, which are learned through focused, intentional practice, eventually result in flawless, automatic execution.

Just as dedicated practice strengthens motor pathways (called "myelination") for a gymnast, so too dedicated moral practice strengthens neuropathways to specific parts of the brain that ignite empathy, kindness, humility, and so forth. When a gymnast decides to move, the primary motor cortex in her brain determines precisely which muscles to activate and with how much force. In the same way, myelinated connections between our cognitive and emotional brains precisely activate the moral and performance muscles required for flawless execution. Intentional, dedicated practice builds moral competence: You are an "athlete" of character.

Be what you want others to become.

For many years at our Institute, we operated a small tennis academy for juniors, aged 9 to 18. The tennis program's goal was to leverage all the demands and stresses of elite junior tennis to build, first and foremost, muscles of character. The objective was to repurpose all the disappointment, hard work, uncertainty, injuries, wins, losses, and more to build in each young athlete muscles of honesty, integrity, respect, humility, kindness, resiliency, and confidence. While the players were myelinating the motor pathways for their forehands, backhands, serves, and volleys, they were also myelinating the character pathways for engagement, generosity, positivity, and gratitude. Each day, players selected a specific Character Muscle they wanted to strengthen. Building the targeted muscle happened by acting it out on court, thinking about it, and writing daily in a character journal. The player's highest priority every day in practice and competition was not winning or achieving a certain strict performance goal but determining who they were becoming because of the demands of tennis. We called our approach "intentional adaptation." Human beings are always adapting to their environments, but sometimes it's to the detriment of their character. Our coaching staff was committed to intentional adaptation, to building character in the players and not allowing their developing character to be hijacked by their pursuit of tennis fame.

The result? Sure, our players became extraordinary competitors as judged by their national rankings and university scholarships – but, far more importantly, they experienced significant character growth as judged by the players themselves, their parents, and their coaches.

As I wrote at the start of this chapter, we human beings love to chase. We frequently don't stop to ask ourselves, mid-chase, critical questions, such as:

1. What am I chasing?

2. Why am I chasing it?

3. Who am I – and who are those I lead – becoming as a consequence of the chase?

The answers to the first two questions are best thought of, from all the evidence, as self-determined, not pre-determined and immutable. These questions bring us face to face with our central purpose for living.

Most important is the third question. When our grand purpose for living is more about serving others than ourselves, or when we focus what we do primarily to serve others, it matters less what we're chasing, or what we do to make a living. In the words of the former tennis great Arthur Ashe, "From what we get, we can make a living; from what we give, we can make a life." Our treatment of others is invariably the calculus we use for becoming our best self. And to make this happen, the muscles of morality can be trained and balanced in the same way that we train physical muscles. Issues of muscle balance, muscle size, synergy, reciprocal inhibition, and the concepts of agonist and antagonist apply to both worlds.

For all sad words of tongue or pen, the saddest are these, "It might have been."—John Greenleaf Whittier

Character Call-Outs

For You   For Work   For Family

KINDNESS/LOVE/CARE FOR OTHERS

Definition: The acquired disposition to have a deep regard and affection for others (Moral Strength).

Self: Commit two acts of kindness each week for the next three weeks and record them in your journal with dates, times, and actions taken. Tell your spouse/partner, children, and so forth, that you love them at least once every day.

Others: (Business) Allow team members to invest half a day each month helping those who are less fortunate. Team members prepare a monthly summary of the community service they invested in. (Family) Have family members report back every Friday on one act of kindness each performed during the week.

Rate Yourself:

1	2	3	4	5

Relatively Weak   Relatively Strong

Character Call-Outs

For You   For Work   For Family

AFFECTION

Definition: The acquired disposition to openly show warmth and caring toward others (Moral Strength).

Self: Openly showing warmth and caring is very difficult for some people. You may feel affection on the inside but unable to show it on the outside. Affection is communicated by both verbal language and body language. Make the commitment to improve your authentic expression of warmth and caring in both word and gesture. Giving hugs, saying "I love you" or "I miss you" can be learned with the conscious intention to do so and the repeated investment of energy in that direction. Keep a record of every investment.

Others: (Business) Discuss the importance of leaders and team members displaying warmth and caring toward each other. Explore how affection and warmth are appropriately communicated in both word and gesture in a business setting. Discuss the importance of being authentic in expression. Explain to team members how regular energy investments will cause growth to occur in this character strength. (Family) Openly displaying affection to family members is a powerful way to strengthen this ability in them. Modeling what you want others to learn is a powerful teacher.

Rate Yourself:

1	2	3	4	5
Relatively Weak				Relatively Strong

CHARACTER CALL-OUTS

For You   For Work   For Family

GRATITUDE

Definition: The acquired disposition to feel a sincere appreciation for what you have (Moral Strength).

Self: Begin or end each day by listing as many things as you can that you can be grateful for in your life. Write your list for 2 minutes in the back of your journal every day. Each day attempt to add things to your gratefulness list that you have never listed before. Read your gratitude journal at the end of each week.

Others: (Business) Begin every monthly team meeting by having team members acknowledge something they are grateful for regarding their work. (Family) Begin each family dinner by having family members mention one thing they are grateful for in their lives.

Rate Yourself:

1	2	3	4	5

Relatively Weak   Relatively Strong

CHARACTER CALL-OUTS

For You   For Work   For Family

COMPASSION

Definition: The acquired disposition to feel a deep, abiding concern for the suffering of others combined with the aspiration to do something to relieve it (Moral Strength).

Self: Compassion for others is rooted in self-compassion. Work first with the tone and content of your self-directed Private Voice. Speak to yourself the way you would speak to someone you care deeply about and speak to others the way you like to be spoken to. Listen carefully to messages of pain, hurt, or discomfort hidden behind the words people are speaking. When you sense such feelings, respectfully acknowledge them. Keep a record of the investments you are intentionally making to expand your capacity for compassion and warmth.

Others: (Business) Questions for team members to discuss and explore: How does compassion relate to our business success? Are compassion for others and competitive success mutually exclusive? What role does compassion have in leadership? (Family) Discuss why compassion for others is important to success in life. Explore why it is important to one's family. Discuss how self-compassion and compassion for others are related. Ask family members how warmth or gentleness is communicated, and ask each to provide concrete examples from his or her world of experience. Ask how they feel when compassion is expressed toward them.

Rate Yourself:

1	2	3	4	5
Relatively Weak				Relatively Strong

Character Call-Outs

For You   For Work   For Family

EMPATHY

Definition: The acquired disposition to experience what others are thinking and feeling (Moral Strength).

Self: Deliberately try to think and feel the way others are. Put yourself in their shoes in terms of the how they think and feel inside. Recount in your journal what you believe the thoughts and feelings are of another person and then attempt to experience those thoughts and feelings in yourself.

Others: (Business) Discuss these questions: How might empathy help you to become a better team member, a better sales person, a better leader? (Family) Discuss how learning to be empathic can help you be a better person, more patient, more caring, more tolerant of others. Have each family member give a specific example of being empathic.

Rate Yourself:

1	2	3	4	5

Relatively Weak   Relatively Strong

CHARACTER CALL-OUTS

For You   For Work   For Family

HUMILITY

Definition: The acquired disposition to be modest and highly aware of one's shortcomings (Moral Strength).

Self: Whenever the opportunity arises, diminish your own contributions and give credit to others. Be quick to credit others and reluctant to take the credit yourself. Keep an accurate record of your efforts.

Others: (Business) Ask team members to write about the role humility plays in leadership. What is the impact of hubris on the team's ability to fulfill its potential? How do team members display humility, and how do they display arrogance? (Family) Ask family members to reflect on the questions: What is humility? Why is it important in life? How do you display it? What does it mean to have a big ego? Why is that a problem?

Rate Yourself:

1	2	3	4	5
Relatively Weak				Relatively Strong

CHARACTER CALL-OUTS

For You   For Work   For Family

FORGIVENESS

Definition: The acquired disposition to clear the record for those who have harmed you (Moral Strength).

Self: The inability to forgive others blocks emotional healing. Toxic negative feelings become trapped and serve to drain one's energy resources. The ability to forgive is learned and returns as much to the forgiver as it does for the person being forgiven. One of the best ways to strengthen the capacity for forgiveness is through the healing power of writing. The work of James Pennebaker is illustrative of the potential positive impact of writing. Spend 5 to 10 minutes of daily writing to (1) dissolve any unresolved pain or hurt and (2) express your desire to achieve genuine forgiveness.

Others: (Business) In the high-stress, high-pressure world of business, office politics can get ugly. People can say and do things that are insensitive and hurtful, and battle lines can be drawn that are quite destructive. Staying positive, non-defensive, and forgiving facilitates team dynamics in an important way. Grudge-holding affords no advantages personally or professionally. Encourage team members to use journal writing to break through emotional barriers that prevent the muscle of forgiveness from strengthening. (Family) Childhood is a great opportunity to build the foundation for forgiveness. Battles between siblings and friends are constantly being waged. Learning how to bounce back quickly from injustices and to forgive the offenders begins to strengthen the all-important capacity for forgiveness. Encourage family members to "forgive and move on" when the urge to hold a grudge arises.

Rate Yourself:

1	2	3	4	5
Relatively Weak				Relatively Strong

Character Call-Outs

For You   For Work   For Family

GENEROSITY

Definition: The acquired disposition to share whatever you have with others (Moral Strength).

Self: Commit at least one act of generosity every week by sharing what you have with others. You can give money, food, clothing, books, or anything that has personal value or your time through providing advice, mentorship, coaching, and so forth. Keep a record.

Others: (Business) Have team members select a new project every two months for expressing their generosity. Team members are to keep a record of their generosity investments. (Family) Set a goal for each family member to perform one act of generosity every week and report back to the family on a specific day of the week.

Rate Yourself:

1	2	3	4	5
Relatively Weak				Relatively Strong

CHAPTER 5

The Bricks and Mortar of Credo-Building

As a human being, you have no choice about the fact that you need a philosophy. Your only choice is whether you define your philosophy by a conscious, rational, disciplined process of thought and scrupulously logical deliberation – or let your subconscious accumulate a junk heap of unwarranted conclusions, false generalizations, undefined contradictions, undigested slogans, unidentified wishes, doubts and fears, thrown together by chance, but integrated by your subconscious into a kind of mongrel philosophy and fused into a single, solid weight: self-doubt, like a ball and chain in the place where your mind's wings should have grown.—Ayn Rand

"Credo" is Latin for "I believe" and refers to a fundamental set of beliefs that guide behaviors. Credos generally come in two forms, organizational and personal. An organizational credo, sometimes referred to as a creed, is a statement of shared beliefs and values. A Personal Credo is an individual statement of beliefs and values. It's important to note that while beliefs are notions we hold to be true, they may or may not have moral ramifications; they represent our interpretation of the world as we have come to experience it. Auditory, visual, and kinesthetic data stream into our neuroprocessing system and must be organized and interpreted for our experiences to make sense; we human beings are, after all, meaning makers. As the raw data stream in, we provide context, structure, and relevance to them. If we can't find a place for certain input – if it is meaningless to our preexisting mental and emotional experience (what's already loaded in and accepted) – then it is discarded, purged, or intentionally altered so that it *does* fit. We experience the sun rising and setting every day; we develop a belief that the sun will rise and set tomorrow. If we don't experience the sun rising or setting, we assume it was cloudy, we slept through it, we simply missed it, or we disregard or purge our observation altogether. That's how we preserve our sanity and a sense of coherence. If the meaning we attribute to our experience and the beliefs that flow from those meanings cannot be properly organized, interpreted, and predicted? We get chaos.

The fact that an opinion has been widely held is no evidence whatever that it is not utterly absurd.—Bertrand Russell, *Marriage and Morals*

Beliefs and the stories that spawn them can be true or not true; they can represent the real world or be completely false. As Andrew Newberg and Mark Waldman aptly put it in their book *Why We Believe What We Believe*, "Beliefs govern nearly every aspect of our lives. They tell us how to pray, how to vote, whom to trust, whom to avoid; they shape our personal behaviors and spiritual ethics throughout life. But once our beliefs are established, we rarely challenge their validity, even when faced with contradictory evidence." Humans once believed that the world was flat, that the Earth was the center of the universe, that disease was caused by evil spirits, that machines could never fly, that traveling to the moon and back was impossible, that cars could never drive themselves, and on and on. Fundamentally, a belief is a state of mind; and the stronger the belief, the more trust and confidence we have that it represents the world as it exists. Some beliefs die hard. Core beliefs are those that we have actively and intentionally thought about and embraced. They become fundamental to how we operate and behave in the world. When one or more of our core beliefs are challenged, or found to be demonstrably untrue, it can be highly disturbing and destabilizing.

When we prioritize our beliefs, we begin to form our values. Beliefs represent our convictions about what we hold to be true; our values prioritize them according to their order of importance. Put another way, beliefs become our roadmap for reality; values become our guide to what's truly important. Just as we have core beliefs, we have core values, which identify the beliefs that represent the very highest priority, such as honesty or respect for others.

As early as 2002, researchers, using a brain imaging technology called functional magnetic resonance imaging (fMRI) found that the left frontal lobe and the left temporal lobe are activated when we make moral judgments. The areas activated are also associated with abstract reasoning, regulation of emotions, and willful thinking.

We might ask: What exactly are these areas of the brain referencing, as we decide to act or not act in a particular way, to summon compassion or tough-mindedness, to take ethical shortcuts or not, to be selfish or selfless? What is the source code the brain is accessing for vetting the moral issues we confront every day? And, of equal importance, where did it come from? Was the source code intentionally and consciously constructed, or did it simply evolve from the forces of life – that is, without much reflection? As noted earlier, most leaders acknowledge that the origin of their core beliefs and values is not entirely clear to them. Their moral source code is not thoughtfully and meticulously self-constructed, but seemed to take form more by itself than through conscious intervention.

As our experience repeatedly teaches us, our moral navigation system possesses serious flaws, yet we continue to trust it to guide us in the most important journey of our lives – namely, "getting home" morally. How do you go from trusting this system to verifying it? From automatically accepting this system to vetting it rigorously, intentionally?

You create a Personal Credo document. This is a very special document – a sacred document, if you will. To create it will take many, many weeks. It will be the standard against which all your moral decisions and judgments are to be vetted. Contained in this document are your soulful reflections and decisions about such things as your Ultimate Mission in life (your core purpose for living), your core beliefs, and core values.

In creating your Personal Credo document, you are adding the necessary level of thoughtfulness, deliberation, and intentionality to strengthening your character so that it is equal to the task of helping you to be your best self and paves the way for your desired legacy.

Organizational Credos

A cadet will not lie, cheat, steal or tolerate those who do.

Virtually every branch of the U.S. military, where the stakes are literally life and death, has constructed a document that defines who they are as a culture, what they do (their Ultimate Mission), and how they are to do it. Credos have been created to improve operational success and esprit de corps among the troops. The Navy SEAL community felt it imperative to turn what was unwritten and revered into a codified, indelible document, so in 2005 a team was assembled to put into words what it meant to be a SEAL – their core beliefs and values.

The SEAL code:

- Loyalty to Country, Team and Teammate
- Serve with Honor and Integrity On and Off the Battlefield
- Ready to Lead, Ready to Follow, Never Quit
- Take Responsibility for Your Actions and the Actions of Your Teammates
- Excel as Warriors Through Discipline and Innovation
- Train for War, Fight to Win, Defeat our Nation's Enemies
- Earn Your Trident Everyday

After considerable reflection, a remarkable document was created that, in just a few phrases and sentences, accomplished several things. The SEAL Code identifies the moral character strengths deemed most critical to the SEAL community: loyalty, honor, integrity. Next, the code identifies the most important performance character strengths: persistence and determination ("never quit"), responsibility, discipline, innovation. Both the moral and performance character strengths in the code speak to *how* a Navy SEAL is to conduct business and complete the mission. It is significant that moral strengths are listed first: The *how* precedes the *what* (winning and defeating the enemy). Put another way, how a Navy SEAL conducts business in protecting the country ranks above what he must do to win and defeat the enemy. Soldiers know there are many paths to winning, but a SEAL will follow only those defined by loyalty, honor, and integrity.

If the establishment of a credo is deemed important enough to prepare soldiers to face life and death battlefield pressure, it's not surprising that companies across the world have adopted the practice. Johnson & Johnson's Credo, General Motors' Code of Ethics, the Ritz Carlton Credo, KPMG's integrity document, Walmart's Credo, Procter & Gamble's document on values-based growth – these are just a very few examples. The Boy Scouts and Girl Scouts have their own Scouts' Law. The Boy Scout law lists 12 character strengths, some moral and some performance:

Trustworthy, loyal, helpful, friendly, courteous, kind, obedient, cheerful, thrifty, brave, clean, and reverent.

A firmly embedded credo doesn't guarantee authentic, responsible, moral behavior, but it significantly improves our chances.

Each credo or creed, in its unique way, prioritizes the values, beliefs, and character strengths to be embodied in that culture. Each credo codifies the moral rules of engagement for conducting its business.

But it's important to note that the success of an organizational credo depends on how much it gets woven into the Personal Credo of each member of that culture. An organizational credo is nothing more than words strung together until it is embedded in the neuroprocessing system of everyone involved. It must become an integral part of a person's Personal Credo for it to have the desired influence over his or her behavior.

How does the embedding process take place? Indoctrination – cultural indoctrination, self-indoctrination, or a combination of both. Indoctrination means to train, teach, instruct, inculcate targeted beliefs, values, doctrines, attitudes, or principles. The indoctrination process occurs with repeated forms of energy investment – writing about it, hearing about it, reading about it, talking about it, thinking about it, visualizing and rehearsing it, and acting it out. *Doing* it. The more such training inputs are used and the higher their frequency and intensity, the faster and more durable the indoctrination. Strong military cultures like West Point, the Naval Academy and the Air Force Academy, religious institutions, sports teams, and even some businesses deploy many or most of the training inputs just mentioned. The objective is always the same: to embed targeted beliefs, values, ways of thinking and acting into the neuroprocessing system of everyone involved. The intent is to have influence in the formation of each individual's Personal Credo.

REFLECTIVE RESISTANCE

Before you begin the process of building your Personal Credo, you must first actively resist the powerful urge to go through this process quickly. If you do, you will not gain its profound benefit.

You will probably want to make haste and get to the bottom line swiftly; that's how many of you got to be where you are and who you are. As leaders, we take pride in getting things done in record time, completed in half the time of our predecessors. Phrases like "under budget" and "ahead of schedule" are music to our ears. The pace of business life today turns legions of leaders into what I call, affectionately, "speed addicts." Management scholar Henry Mintzberg, after intensively investigating the day-to-day activities of managers nearly 50 years ago, concluded that "activities are characterized by brevity, variety, and discontinuity and that they are strongly oriented to action and dislike reflective activities." And he discovered this to be the case nearly half a century ago! What multiplier would we use to reflect the unreal pace of business life today? Taking precious time for conscious reflection in today's business world has, unfortunately, become increasingly counter-cultural. In building a Personal Credo and in making sound moral judgments, going fast virtually assures failure.

So before you undertake the construction of what will likely be the single most important navigational document in your life, the document against which all your moral judgments will be vetted, please consider the following:

1. Personal Credo–building is deliberative and intentional. This thoughtful process requires you to set aside time in a quiet location to build and refine this document. If you speed through the steps little, if anything, will come of it. Remember: Three to six weeks of dedicated training are required to increase the strength of physical muscles of the body. Strengthening character muscles and building the neurological architecture (neuropathways) supportive of those muscles take time, as well. Reading this chapter is but one training input. Writing down your first answers is another. Constructing a Personal Credo built to last and strong enough to withstand the forces of life simply cannot be done quickly. It will become a lifelong process of refining, recalibrating, re-evaluating. We must fight our inner urge to go fast, resist the temptation to get it done and get on to the next thing. Failure to allow sufficient time for intentional, soulful, reflective pauses guarantees failure to lead with character.

2. The document you are about to create is the lens through which every moral decision may be vetted. Because your Personal Credo represents the clearest, most accurate, self-determined articulation of your core beliefs, core values, mission, and purpose in life, it becomes your ultimate source code for determining right from wrong, for navigating the moral storms of life.

3. Your Personal Credo is your best effort to rise above any flawed familial, cultural, or religious inputs, to transcend blind spots, sloppy thinking, faulty values and beliefs, to rigorously confront character weaknesses and imbalances, and to assume full responsibility for all decisions that impact your treatment of others.

4. Your Personal Credo is not a written document to be used as a reference guide. It is designed to be embedded at the core

of your neuroprocessing system. It needs to become the centerpiece of your worldview, your ultimate reality, your core mindset. It is to become nothing short of your internalized roadmap for a truly successful life.

5. Your Personal Credo represents the scorecard of highest value to you. When you score well, as measured by the dictates of this document, it means your life is fundamentally aligned with who you most aspire to be, with your Best Moral Self.

Many live a long life and never have an intentionally crafted Personal Credo to guide them.

MISSION CONTROL CENTRAL

A useful analogy for many of our clients at the Institute is the nearby Mission Control Center at Cape Canaveral, Florida. The Kennedy Space Center is only 30 miles east of our training center, and many of the Center's space launches are visible from our location, particularly the night launches. Whether manned or unmanned, all space launches are under the Agency's Mission Control operation. The ultimate supervisor of each space launch is the Flight Director. All decisions regarding orbit entrance and exit, go or no-go, management of emergencies, abort decisions, and countless other choices come under his or her authority. Three rows of controllers monitor specific areas of flight operations and keep the Flight Director aware of any concerning deviations from the norm – potential problems with booster systems, capsule communication systems, guidance systems, flight dynamics, retrofire systems, astronaut health, and so on. Controllers monitor trajectories, thermal levels, electrical and mechanical systems, telemetry, lighting, oxygen levels, fuel consumption rates, and much more. Good decisions by the Flight Director and the Mission Control team require careful monitoring of all relevant flight data. Faulty data streams or failure to monitor incoming data streams could spell catastrophe for the mission.

The Personal Credo analogy: You are the Flight Director. You control all decisions relative to the mission, which is to live a life of the highest possible moral character; to lead with character at work and at home; to leave a legacy that will have a meaningful impact on others. Mission success is completely in your hands. You accept total responsibility for the outcome. Data monitors completely fill your Control Center, and you remain open to all feedback and input relevant to the mission. Prior to launch, all flight operations and monitors are pre-loaded with precise guidance coordinates, pertinent tracking data, ideal trajectories, and specific destination parameters. That pre-loaded information takes the form of a single document called Personal Credo. Alarms signal deviation from the norm, anything that might threaten mission success. Instruments signal when there's a threat to core values and core beliefs (i.e., they may be compromised) or when moral and performance character muscles should be deployed. There is round-the-clock monitoring of levels of integrity, honesty, kindness,

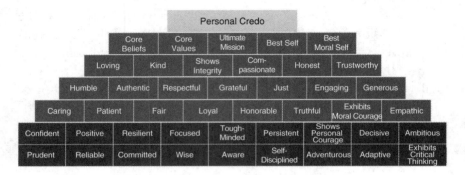

Credo Building Blocks

authenticity, justice, gratitude, and so on. Same for tough-mindedness, positivity, confidence, persistence, and other performance character assets.

(The graphic does not show a complete list. Note that the bottom two rows are Performance Character Strengths and the three rows above them are Ethical/Moral Character Strengths.)

Again: As Flight Director, you decide which moral capabilities should be activated, with how much force, and at what time. Input from both your cognitive brain and emotional brain must be integrated and synchronized. Because moral decision-making and acting in accordance with those decisions requires energy, matters such as food intake, sleep cycles, movement, hydration levels and the like will also be monitored in the Control Center. Red alerts are signaled when blind spots, faulty thinking, defensiveness, contradictions, misalignments, mistaken assumptions, and other distortions that threaten the mission are detected. Low blood sugar levels, toxic self-talk, rigid or inflexible thinking, or consistently underperforming Character Muscles, like integrity or humility, will be tagged for immediate corrective work. And just as there is for acquiring flight control competence at Kennedy Space Center, there is a steep learning curve for being able to responsibly and effectively manage all the mission-critical variables that surface. The mission targeted in your

Personal Credo will take a lifetime to complete. Yet, excitingly, every single day represents one more opportunity to improve your flight control skills.

COACHING YOU THROUGH THE CREDO-BUILDING PROCESS

Let's start with a commitment that involves two investments: energy and time.

Energy means bringing your absolute best effort to each daily thinking and writing exercise. Time means investing a minimum of 10 minutes every day for the duration of the training. A minimum investment of 90 days is required to get this mission off the launch pad; another 60 days is required to ensure success. Yes, I hear you: I'm fully aware you already have no time in your life for anything new. But isn't one of the hallmarks of a leader the ability to see what really matters? To see the bigger picture? Because of the critical nature of this mission – nothing less than the success of your life – it's imperative to find the energy and time to make it happen; indeed, it should rise to the level of "no-brainer" more than virtually any other challenge currently facing you. My recommendation is for you to awaken 10 minutes earlier than you normally do, and get the work completed before the demands of life descend on you. Much of the training will be writing. We want to form a daily habit – or a ritual, as we at the Institute call it – for pre-planned self-reflection.

From our nearly three decades of experience, it takes 20 to 60 days, on average, to form a habit. For some, the first 7 days of this training are particularly tough. Anticipate and accept any discomfort when it comes, and just expect that, as with the building of physical muscle, you're unlikely to notice tangible results for the first couple of weeks or even more. Eventually, a shift takes place, and rather than your feeling as if you're forcing yourself to do the exercises, you will be drawn to them. Eventually, you'll actually start missing it when you fail to work it into your daily routine.

So: The training process begins when you commit to invest your full, best energy for 10 minutes a day.

Caution: Your Private Voice may try to convince you to abort the mission, describing it as a "waste of time," a "boondoggle," "too touchy-feely." Disregard this negative messaging. Continue forward. Nothing of value happens easily; almost always you need to push into discomfort for real growth to occur. Again, think of how you feel when you're strengthening your physical muscles.

- The writing topics for each of the first 90 days and the following 60 days are pre-determined, and the schedule must be maintained. If the assignment for Day 27 is missed, find the time to make it up. The creation of your Personal Credo should be completed in as close to 90 days as possible. It is fine for you to write longer than 10 minutes – and some exercises are meant to be completed over multiple days – but 10 minutes is the minimum required for each day. Avoid completing multiple assignments at one time, or on the same day. Business travel, vacation days, personal emergencies should not exempt you from your training. If you miss a day or two, make up the assignments as soon as you can and do your best to stay on schedule.

You may wish to have your spouse or partner go through the daily journaling exercises and compare notes from time to time.

For those working with an executive coach: If you are unsure about a question or struggling with the exercise in some other way, make a note to discuss it with your coach. We also recommend checking in with your coach regularly to discuss key learning and insights.

Finally: You may wonder why examples of Personal Credos from our clients have not been provided here or in the accompanying journal. Experience has shown us that examples have too much influence over our thinking. Rather than creating something completely original and authentic, we pick and choose what we like from the work of others. A Personal Credo must be uniquely crafted in a way that you alone could author. It can be 1 paragraph or 10, specific or general. This sacred document must be totally your creation.

Remember: a minimum of 10 minutes per day.

That's it.

Good luck, on arguably the most important journey of your life.

CHARACTER CALL-OUTS

For You   For Work   For Family

TRUST

Definition: The acquired disposition to believe in the basic goodness of others (Moral Strength).

Self: When one's basic trust in others has been seriously violated, the trust muscle may be seriously weakened. A weak muscle of trust can take the form of pervasive suspicion. You never allow people to get too close to you to avoid being hurt or taken advantage of. Everyone is seen through the prism of distrust. Unfortunately, a weak muscle of trust undermines all human relationships and seriously compromises personal fulfillment and happiness. The fact is, not all people are untrustworthy, and not all people are trustworthy. Both the muscles of trust and discernment should be worked to provide protection from being taken advantage of. The damage done to one's life from distrusting everyone is far greater than the occasional pain experienced when trust is broken. Make a conscious choice to build your trust muscle knowing full well that you will occasionally be let down. Trust is a choice and, when combined with a strong muscle of discernment, minimizes the risk of being hurt. When a trust issue arises, assume the goodness in others but keep your discernment muscle active.

Others: (Business) Learning who you can trust and who you can't is a big factor in business success. Without trust in others, virtually all business transactions are doomed to failure. Discuss the meaning of "trust but verify" as it relates to business. Explore the importance of balancing strengths of trust and discernment in operating a successful business. (Family) Explore the following questions in a family meeting: (1) Can you be trusted? (2) Do you trust others? (3) What are the consequences for losing trust in people? (4) Why do people lose their trust in others? (5) How can you trust in others and still minimize being hurt or let down?

Rate Yourself:

1	2	3	4	5
Relatively Weak				Relatively Strong

Character Call-Outs

For You   For Work   For Family

LOYALTY

Definition: The acquired disposition to be faithful to one's friends, family, and associates (Moral Strength).

Self: Write in your journal about what loyalty means to you and why it has value in your life. Think about times in your life when someone you cared about was disloyal to you. How did you feel? Recall an example of someone displaying great loyalty to you. Describe what that was like. Give examples of where you might be able to grow your loyalty muscle in your everyday interactions. Keep an accurate record of your efforts.

Others: (Business) Discuss what loyalty means in leadership and what role it plays in business success. Discuss how loyalty must be balanced with justice. Provide examples of loyalty and disloyalty. (Family) Ask all family members to provide an example of someone being faithful and loyal to them. How did it make them feel? Why do people become disloyal?

Rate Yourself:

1	2	3	4	5
Relatively Weak				Relatively Strong

CHARACTER CALL-OUTS

For You   For Work   For Family

DEPENDABILITY

Definition: The acquired disposition to be counted on to meet your commitments (Moral Strength).

Self: Dependability is a supportive muscle to integrity – you do what you say you will do. It is also a supportive muscle to trustworthiness. When people can't depend on you, they can't trust you. A weak dependability muscle also reflects a lack of respect for others. To build this muscle, design a dependability log that records every promise and commitment you make to others and whether you were responsible in meeting them. Strive each week for improvement.

Others: (Business) Have team members give concrete examples of both not being dependable and being dependable, and the effects of each on the team's functioning. Have team members brainstorm how the muscle of dependability could be strengthened for their team. (Family) Have each family member mention one thing in the last week that they did that supported being dependable and anything they might have done to undermine it. Talk about the consequences for being undependable in life. Discuss practical ways to build the muscle such as journaling, goal setting, and doing.

Rate Yourself:

1	2	3	4	5
Relatively Weak				Relatively Strong

CHARACTER CALL-OUTS

For You For Work For Family

PATIENCE WITH OTHERS

Definition: The acquired disposition to accept imperfections in others (Moral Strength).

Self: Patience is a form of respect for others. Accepting the imperfections in others embraces their humanity. Human beings are imperfect regardless of their commitment to perfection or their level of natural talent. The muscle of patience is supported by muscles of warmth, caring, and respect for others. Just saying the word "patience" when the impulse arises to be critical or judgmental can become a powerful tool for strengthening this muscle. Saying the word "patience" takes you back to your values and rallies willpower and self-control.

Others: (Business) Discuss how patience for others is evidenced on your team. Explore its relevance to effective leadership. Discuss the difference between patience for others and lowering performance standards. Where does intolerance of ethical violations fall? (Family) Have each family member give an example of patience for others from his or her own life. Explore the relationship between the muscle of patience and the muscle of respect for others. Explore what it feels like when people you care about are impatient with you.

Rate Yourself:

1	2	3	4	5

Relatively Weak   Relatively Strong

CHARACTER CALL-OUTS

For You   For Work   For Family

RESPECT FOR OTHERS

Definition: The acquired disposition to treat everyone with dignity (Moral Strength).

Self: Say an enthusiastic "good morning" to everyone you meet. Be fully engaged whenever you meet others. Good eye contact and positive gestures are reflections of respect.

Others: (Business) Start all staff meetings by acknowledging everyone present and thank them for attending the meeting. Allow everyone to have a chance to express their thoughts and feelings. (Family) Encourage your children to say, "Thank you," open doors for others, and send thank you notes.

Rate Yourself:

1	2	3	4	5

Relatively Weak   Relatively Strong

Character Call-Outs

For You   For Work   For Family

PUNCTUALITY

Definition: The acquired disposition to honor time commitments (Performance Strength).

Self: Set a goal to be 5 minutes early for every appointment or time commitment. Be sure to link your being on time to your core values such as respect for others or integrity. Keep a precise daily log of your results.

Others: (Business) As a leader, set the value proposition that punctuality is an importance character strength for the team. Expect everyone to arrive a few minutes early for every team meeting. Start meetings on time and finish on time – and schedule 25- and 50-minute meetings to give attendees time for a quick recovery break and the ability to make it on time to the next meeting. Make note of everyone who is consistently late and establish consequences. (Family) Discuss how punctuality connects to respect for others, integrity, and overall success in life. Have each family member report back on punctuality at the end of the week. Each must check "on-time" or "not on-time" for all time commitments for the week. Encourage everyone to be at least 5 minutes early for every commitment.

Rate Yourself:

1	2	3	4	5
Relatively Weak				Relatively Strong

CHARACTER CALL-OUTS

For You   For Work   For Family

VITALITY / VIGOR

Definition: The acquired disposition to feel energetic, to feel enthusiasm for life (Performance Strength).

Self: Everyone has an energy signature. Vitality is expressed in enthusiasm, passion, and excitement. High positive energy is attractive in others and is contagious. Raising one's energy signature is a two-step process. Step 1 is ensuring energy reserves are as high as possible – eating right, sleeping right, proper rest, exercise, and so forth. Step 2 is finding ways to express high positive energy in body language, verbal expression, and communication style. Use video replay in learning how you can naturally express more positive energy. Grade yourself on your expression of vitality and vigor.

Others: (Business) Ask team members to explore the importance of energy in leadership. Ask them to look at their own energy signature. Is it high or low, positive or negative? Discuss the statement "Leaders lead first and foremost with their energy." Explore how energy reserves are built and the importance of body language and communication style. (Family) Ask family members to give examples of high-energy and low-energy people they know. Which do they prefer and why? Discuss whether they feel one's energy signature can be raised. Discuss how actors and actresses in film and stage are able to do it. Discuss where energy comes from – food, movement, rest, sleep, hydration, and so on, and the role of body language and verbal expression.

Rate Yourself:

1	2	3	4	5
Relatively Weak				Relatively Strong

CHARACTER CALL-OUTS

For You   For Work   For Family

SELF-AWARENESS

Definition: The acquired disposition to have reality-based perceptions of one's self (Performance Strength).

Self: Self-awareness powerfully assists us in self-regulation and self-control. Without self-awareness, acting morally ceases to exist. Self-control cannot be learned in any given area without self-awareness. Self-awareness can be enhanced by keeping track of things you want to control. Quantifying everything from hours of sleep to the frequency of positive thoughts increases awareness in those areas. In any area of your life where you want to increase awareness, from humility to compassion, quantify its occurrence in your life on a daily basis. Writing daily in your journal enhances self-awareness in a dynamic way.

Others: (Business) Explain the importance of self-awareness in self-control, self-regulation, and effective leadership. Have team members increase awareness through quantification in some important aspect of their business performance. For example, recording how much time each team member spends talking versus listening to clients creates awareness of listening skills. Discuss how a lack of self-awareness is evidenced on a daily basis in business. Explain how quantification can be used to increase self-awareness in any aspect of one's business life and how awareness is the first step in advancing self-control. Quantifying how much time one spends on telephone calls, on paperwork, on being frustrated with office politics, on total hours of sleep, represents an important step in advancing self-regulation in those areas. (Family) Have a discussion on how and why self-awareness is important to success in life. Discuss how a lack of self-awareness is evidenced on a daily basis. Quantifying how much time one spends watching TV, playing video games, cell phone use, connecting on social media, and so forth represents an important step in advancing self-regulation in those areas. Encourage family members to keep a record to exercise greater control.

Rate Yourself:

1	2	3	4	5
Relatively Weak				Relatively Strong

Chapter 6

Embedding Your Personal Credo and Supporting It with Habits

If I always appear prepared, it is because before entering an undertaking, I have meditated long and have foreseen what might occur. It is not genius that reveals to me suddenly and secretly what I should do in circumstances unexpected by others; it is thought and preparation.—Napoleon Bonaparte

For the first 90 days of your training, you will be thoughtfully birthing your Personal Credo in the journal that accompanies this book. Day by day, word by word, your source code for judging right from wrong will take form. Whether you fully realize it or not, the brief 10-minute daily reflections, spread over three months, will steadily change the way your brain functions in moral situations and in who you become as a person and a leader. Repeated investments of your energy will begin to influence what you think, do, say, even feel.

The second, 60-day phase of your training is also crucial: This is when you operationalize and habituate the work you did in the first 90 days. The same investment of 10-minute daily reflections, recorded in your personal journal, are designed to accomplish two things:

1. More deeply embed your Personal Credo into your neurological architecture (self-indoctrination).

2. Create as many habits as possible to support the *automatic* implementation of your Personal Credo, when time does not allow for more deliberate reflection (e.g., as soon as you enter moral territory relating to thinking, decisions, and behavior, the words "integrity" and "honesty" are immediately triggered).

The embedding process will occur naturally in your daily writing assignment, but habit building requires more explanation and understanding.

As creatures of habit, our everyday life is dominated by responses that occur automatically – that is, without conscious intervention. Think about how much of your day is about habit: the time you wake and go to bed, the side of the bed you sleep on, your personal hygiene routine, the route you take to work, where you put your keys, how and when you exercise, where you watch TV, and on and on and on. Imagine how difficult life would be if every action, such as moving your hand back and forth to brush your teeth or raising your hand to drink a glass of water, required conscious, intentional oversight. Once the habit of brushing your teeth is imprinted neurologically, we can focus on something entirely different, with no diminishment to the automatic action. Some habits are intentionally created – wearing a seatbelt, eating certain foods, arriving five minutes early for appointments – and some just start showing up. Non-intentional habits might include having a bowl of ice cream before going to bed or smoking cigarettes.

Some habits are helpful; some clearly aren't. Good habits support our self-control resources and help us manage our energy. Habits allow us to conserve energy for important things that either aren't or can't be habituated. Once established, habits generate neurological cravings that make the breaking of habits – including extremely harmful ones – very challenging. Neuroscience has helped us understand that, rather than breaking habits, we are actually conditioning a new response to the same stimulus.

Have you ever noticed how the best tennis players in the world use structured rituals over and over between points? Have you ever wondered what they're doing? (You'll also notice this with pitchers and batters in baseball before each pitch, with placekickers in football before they kick, with free-throw shooters in basketball before each attempt, etc.) In the early 1980s, I developed a training system designed to help tennis players use the 25-second period between points to their maximum competitive advantage. That same system continues to be used by tennis coaches around the world to teach mental toughness. The objective of the training was to assist players in developing the physical, emotional, and mental habits *between* points that supported their ability to perform at their best *during* points, to enter what I called their "ideal performance state." I came to realize that the precious seconds between points represented an invaluable, ever-present, well-regulated opportunity for players to reboot physically, emotionally, and mentally before the next point. With proper training and discipline, anger could be dissolved into calmness, frustration into positivity, distraction into laser focus . . . literally within seconds. With between-point habits in place, players could automatically re-enter their ideal performance state before the start of the next point.

Training the right habits between points began by having players create, in effect, their between-point credo – who they wanted to be as a competitor. Next, they had to decide how they wanted to respond to mistakes, to opponents who cheat, to hostile crowds, fatigue, score pressure, and so on. Targeted *emotional* responses included calmness, positivity, confidence, present focus, enjoyment, and 100% effort. Targeted *physical* responses included shoulders back and broad, confident walk (I called it "the matador walk"), eye control – on the racquet strings or on the ground (wandering eyes lead to a wandering mind), muscles relaxed, and deep breathing. Once players knew how they wanted to respond, the next step was to train those responses until they became habits – until they occurred automatically.

At our Institute, we employ this same process for strengthening moral competency. Examples might include a daily gratitude writing exercise for 3 minutes first thing every morning, or a kindness meditation for 4 minutes every night before bed.

Two important differences exist, however, between competitive competency and moral competency.

First, and most obviously: Failure to summon the right response(s) in sports may translate into losing a match or playing badly; failure to summon the right moral response can have catastrophic consequences for ourselves, our families, and the organizations we represent, with ramifications that can last far, far longer than the sting of a loss or a poorly played game.

Second: There is no standard 25-second period, which happens every minute or so, to summon the targeted Credo response. Our response time ranges from just a few seconds to multiple days.

The key to building new habits is investing our energy with consistency and precision.

For nearly three decades, we've taught our clients how to build new, targeted habits in exercise, nutrition, and performance psychology. They learn basic skills and constructs that help them develop positive habits. They understand that

- Habits are formed through repeated investments of energy. This applies to motor habits such as serving a tennis ball, emotional habits such as feeling challenged and optimistic, mental habits such as thinking certain thoughts or words, and moral habits such as doing the right thing, telling the truth, or showing kindness.

- Energy investment spawns growth in the connection between a stimulus and a more instinctual response.

- Energy investments can be made, as has been pointed out, by doing, thinking, talking, visualizing, writing, and feeling. Every investment of energy creates a neurological trace; with repeated investment, this trace is transformed into a reliable neurological pathway. Every time an action or thought is repeated, the connections between neurons are strengthened. Neuropsychologist Donald Hebb puts it succinctly: "Neurons that fire together wire together."

- To *build a new habit*, go there frequently, in precisely the same way with your energy; to *break a habit*, cut off the energy supply by not going there, by investing your energy elsewhere.

The habit-building process we employ at the Institute can be summarized by the formula $H = PTR^3$:

1. H = the Habit we wish to acquire.

2. P = Purpose. When the habit we wish to build is in alignment with our core purpose and values, we are more likely to make the necessary withdrawals from our energy reserves to build the habit.

3. T = Trigger word or cue. A stimulus must connect to a response.

4. R^1 = Response. We wish to make the desired habit response be automatic.

5. R^2 = Reward. A positive payoff is needed to complete the habit loop. Any feel-good experience – fulfillment, joy, happiness, self-satisfaction, self-gratification, pleasure, and so on – will suffice.

6. R^3 = Repetition. Repetition strengthens the connection between stimulus and response.

To demonstrate how this works, let's apply the formula to create the habit of daily journal writing.

In this case, H is for the Habit of journal writing for a minimum of 10 minutes every day.

P is the Purpose driving the daily investments. It represents the "why" behind our desire to do the daily writing exercises. The more clear, powerful, and meaningful the "why," the likelier it is that we will continue to make the energy investments required to form the habit.

T is for the Trigger to start the sequence. This can be you setting your alarm 10 minutes earlier than usual each morning to allow you time to write.

The alarm – the trigger – goes off. Next to the alarm is your personal journal. After turning off the alarm, you immediately pick up your journal and start writing until the 10-minute writing exercise is complete. Picking up your journal and writing in it is the second trigger.

R^1 is the actual response of writing in the journal.

R^2 is the reward you feel for having done the writing. Even though the writing may have stirred some uncomfortable thoughts and feelings, the fact that you completed the writing, which is linked to a deeply important purpose, a sense of fulfillment typically surfaces. Positive feeling becomes a reward.

R^3 is the repetition of the sequence until the habit of daily writing is fully established. You will know the habit is formed when you are pulled to do it, feel something is missing when you don't, and when little or no conscious effort is needed to get you to write. The following graphic summarizes the habit acquisition process.

$$H = PTR^3$$

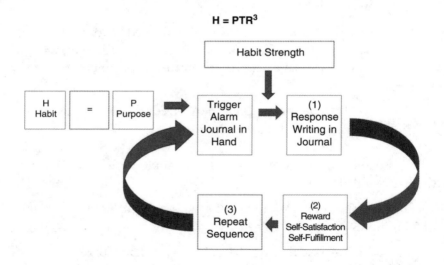

When you're ready, begin the second phase of training, which involves 10 minutes of writing in the accompanying journal, for Days 91–150.

TWO REAL-LIFE CASE STUDIES

Roger, a sales manager, has been journaling for months. He walks into his sales meeting and immediately becomes aware that several members of his team seem edgy, distracted, and nervous – maybe even hostile.

Simultaneously, he picks up feelings of defensiveness, impatience, and irritability in himself. Two days prior to the sales meeting, he had sent out an email suggesting that the team's sub-par performance in the last two months was due, in part, to their sub-par effort and focus. Roger has been taking a lot of heat from his boss for his team's poor numbers. He likes to think of himself as a "tough guy" when it comes to getting his people to meet their performance standards, particularly with sales quotas. Roger's last three performance reviews indicated weakness in humility, kindness, patience, and compassion. Because of the consistent negative evaluation from his boss and direct reports, he made a strong commitment to himself and his boss to do everything he could do to address the weaknesses. For the last several weeks, Roger has not only been doing his 10-minute daily writing, but he has also selected one of his weak muscles, compassion, to write about in his journal every day. He has addressed questions like, "Why is compassion important for me?" "How can I show compassion today?" "What does compassion feel like?"

Following the writing, Roger visualized and rehearsed what he had just written about. His additional writing was recorded in the blank pages at the back of his journal.

Because of the character-building training that Roger was doing, he now realized that this meeting with his team represented an excellent opportunity to activate the character muscles he had been working so hard on. Uncharacteristically, he asked his team members to talk freely about what was going on with them. A barrage of negativity and frustration was directed at Roger. For the team, the big issue was Roger's accusatory and insensitive email. As team members began expressing their displeasure, Roger became acutely aware of his vigorous desire to defend his decision to write the email.

Instead, he listened attentively and continued to encourage feedback. As team members spoke, Roger became aware – consciously aware, that is, fully aware of being aware – that his aggressive, hostile feelings were starting to fade. As he listened to their feelings, explanations, and fears, he began internally to experience *their* feelings rather than being consumed by his own. Eventually, the group dynamics turned from griping and complaining to constructive solutions and possible action. Upon reflection after the meeting, Roger realized he had broken new ground with himself. His targeted 10-minute daily writings enabled him to respond in a way that was entirely uncommon for him.

Have you ever felt like Roger? Have you ever had a boss that behaved like him?

Carol is one person to those she leads at work, and quite another to herself. She is fully aware that her Public and Private Voices rarely speak the same language. Her Public Voice is typically kind and respectful, but her Private Voice – as Carol acknowledges to herself – is brutal, crafting an entirely different message, in a very different tone. She admits that she would be embarrassed and horrified if others could hear what her often-toxic Private Voice was saying. She struggles with Imposter Syndrome, an agonizing condition that makes her feel that she is not as capable or smart as others believe her to be. As a result, she can't let others know the real Carol because, according to her, that person is a fraud.

Evaluations of Carol's performance are consistently positive. She is an exceptionally hard worker and typically succeeds at whatever project she leads. She did get feedback from her team that she is somewhat distant and hard to get to know. One direct report referred to her as "vanilla," another as "too scripted." None of her direct reports feel strongly connected to her because, from their perspective, she doesn't let anyone get close enough to really know her. Carol's 360-degree scores on authenticity and personal confidence have been consistently low compared to her other competencies. Because of the feedback, particularly the comments by her team (which she found quite disturbing), Carol decided to target the character muscles of confidence and authenticity for growth. Part of her training was to become acutely aware of the tone and content of her Private Voice, and to record what she found in the back pages of her journal. When the voice was not constructive and helpful, she was to build a new habit of immediately saying "STOP" to herself, then initiating a self-narrative more aligned with her values and best self.

Like Roger, Carol committed to writing in her personal journal for a minimum of 10 minutes every day for 150 days. To build her confidence muscle, she wrote in the back of her journal about what she wanted her Private Voice to say to her when feelings of insecurity and inferiority surfaced. Rather than being a relentless critic, her Private Voice was to be converted into a constructive inner coach. She was to repeatedly write about what her Private Voice was to say and when it was to say it. The enabler for changing Carol's Inner Voice coaching was – as it was for Roger – personal awareness.

Carol used her daily writing to rehearse how she would speak to someone she deeply cared about who was struggling with the same issues, and commit to following the same inner script. As to her authenticity, Carol worked hard to increase her awareness and to acknowledge when a discrepancy existed between her Public and Private Voices. She attempted consciously to align both voices as much as possible when communicating with others; the goal was transparency and genuineness. Her efforts, whether successful or not, were to be recorded in her journal, with comments.

Over time, Carol's training efforts began to pay off. (Both Roger and Carol, whose names have been changed to protect their privacy, were actual clients at our Institute.) Carol's ability to pause between the stimulus and response, enabled by the daily writing, opened the possibility of an entirely new, uncommon response. Both her confidence and authenticity scores improved significantly.

CHARACTER CALL-OUTS

For You   For Work   For Family

RESILIENCY

Definition: The acquired disposition to bounce back from disappointment or loss (Performance Strength).

Self: Resiliency is evidenced by speed of recovery. It is also a measure of capacity – physically, emotionally, mentally, and spiritually. The faster one recovers (returns to baseline levels), the greater the capacity. Resiliency is an indication of one's speed of healing. Just as speed of one's heart rate recovery after a dose of exercise stress is a measure of physical capacity, so also is speed of recovery emotionally, mentally, and spiritually a measure of capacity in these areas. Recovery emotionally occurs when positive emotions return, recovery mentally occurs when one is successful in refocusing on things not associated with the stressful event, and recovery spiritually occurs when one successfully reignites cherished values, beliefs, and principles. Anytime one expends energy in strengthening the mechanisms of recovery, resiliency is strengthened.

Others: (Business) Help team members find routines for enhancing recovery following stressful events. Examples would include a specific routine for handling a disturbing call with an important client such as getting up from your desk, going for a walk, eating a healthy snack, and hydrating. The important thing is to not take the next call until you are back to baseline levels of positivity, calm, and optimism. (Family) Discuss with family members how resiliency is built in life – stress exposure followed by recovery. Have each family member write down their best strategies for achieving recovery physically, emotionally, mentally, and spiritually for the next family meeting.

Rate Yourself:

1	2	3	4	5
Relatively Weak				Relatively Strong

CHARACTER CALL-OUTS

For You   For Work   For Family

ADAPTABILITY

Definition: The acquired disposition to adjust well to changing conditions (Performance Strength).

Self: Change can be threatening on many levels. The ability to adjust and even invite change is an acquired capacity that is nearly indispensable in today's ever-changing world. Change demands new growth, new mindsets, new habits. Adaptability, survivability, happiness, and longevity are all connected. Resisting or fearing change anchors us to the past. Every time you feel yourself resisting or fearing change, say to yourself, "Change is good for me – I am open to it – bring it on!"

Others: (Business) Discuss how adaptability and team success are linked. What does it mean to be adaptable, and what is its role in leadership? Discuss practically how team members can become more adaptive. (Family) Help family members recognize how fast the world is changing and how unhappy they will be if they can't adapt to change. Have each family member describe a change he or she is facing that requires constructive adaptation. Explain how everyone has choices. You can curse change, hate it, be frustrated by it, or adapt to it. The choice is yours. Choosing to constructively adapt strengthens this critical character trait.

Rate Yourself:

1	2	3	4	5
Relatively Weak				Relatively Strong

CHARACTER CALL-OUTS

For You   For Work   For Family

OPEN-MINDEDNESS

Definition: The acquired disposition to be receptive to new ideas and thoughts (Performance Strength).

Self: Hardening of the arteries in the physical body has a close relative mentally. It's called hardening of the categories. Without constant strengthening of the character muscle of being open-minded, our receptivity to new ideas and thoughts continues to shrink with age. Just as we lose flexibility physically as we age, so also do we lose flexibility emotionally, mentally, and even spiritually without proper training. Open-mindedness is mental flexibility and can be maintained and expanded by consciously investing energy in being receptive to ideas and thoughts different from our own. Every time you do so, every time you resist the impulse to become defensive or closed to new thinking, your open-minded character muscle is stimulated.

Others: (Business) Being open-minded is a prerequisite to innovation and creativity. When teams or organizations become close-minded, trouble is not far behind. Being closed to new thinking is the kiss of death in today's fast-changing business world. Generally speaking, the more success people have, the less open they are to explore new ways of thinking. Close-mindedness can easily become arrogance. Leaders must constantly work the open-minded muscle in themselves and those they are leading. Create discussions, review case studies, challenge your people to expand their limits in being receptive to new thinking. (Family) Have a family discussion on the difference between being open-minded and being close-minded. Have each family member give examples of both. Discuss how one can be open-minded and still be morally strong. Explore how open-mindedness is an important character strength for success in life.

Rate Yourself:

1	2	3	4	5
Relatively Weak				Relatively Strong

CHARACTER CALL-OUTS

For You   For Work   For Family

LOVE OF LEARNING

Definition: The acquired disposition to find joy in discovering new things (Performance Strength).

Self: Make the commitment to spend a minimum of 30 minutes per week in learning something entirely new for its own sake. The objective is to simply find joy and satisfaction in the learning process itself. Examples might include learning to play a musical instrument, learning to draw, reading the classics, or exploring an area of science you were always curious about.

Others: (Business) Encourage team members to have a rich life of learning completely separate from their jobs. At the beginning of every monthly staff meeting, ask for a volunteer to talk briefly about what they are learning that has nothing to do with his or her job. Have them discuss the satisfaction or joy experienced from the activity and whether it helps balance the stress of work. (Family) Each family member must pick a topic he or she would like to learn more about. The sole purpose of the project is to get each person to experience joy in learning something new. All family members report back to the group in three weeks and describe their experiences.

Rate Yourself:

1   **2**   **3**   **4**   **5**

Relatively Weak   Relatively Strong

CHARACTER CALL-OUTS

For You   For Work   For Family

CREATIVITY

Definition: The acquired disposition to generate original, spontaneous thinking and solutions (Performance Strength).

Self: Spend at least 30 minutes each week reading books on creativity and practice the recommended exercises.

Others: (Business) Set aside one hour per month for team members to creatively solve existing business challenges. There is no agenda except finding creative solutions. All solutions are recorded by a scribe. (Family) List major challenges facing the family, such as too little time together, kids constantly fighting, poor grades in school, and so on. Challenge each family member to offer a creative solution to one of the family problems each week and offer an incentive for the best solution.

Rate Yourself:

1	2	3	4	5
Relatively Weak				Relatively Strong

CHARACTER CALL-OUTS

For You For Work For Family

POSITIVITY

Definition: The acquired disposition to view the world through the eyes of opportunity rather than survival (Performance Strength).

Self: Increasing the strength of one's positivity muscle begins with the intention to do exactly that. Keep a record of the number of times you consciously resisted becoming negative or pessimistic in your thinking by sustaining an opportunistic, positive perspective. Your goal is to actively work your positivity muscle at least twice daily for three weeks.

Others: (Business) Have an observer record the ratio of positive versus negative comments by team members during a typical meeting, for instance, two positives to seven negatives, three positives to two negatives, and so on. Researchers have concluded that a minimum ratio of three positives to one negative is required for teams to function effectively. Set a goal for the team to achieve the minimum ratio of three to one. (Family) Researchers have found that for marriages to be successful, a minimum ratio of five positives to one negative is required. That means that for every negative comment that is made, five positive ones must follow to neutralize the potential toxic effect on the relationship.

Rate Yourself:

1	2	3	4	5
Relatively Weak				Relatively Strong

CHARACTER CALL-OUTS

For You   For Work   For Family

HUMOR

Definition: The acquired disposition to laugh at oneself and the ironies of life (Performance Strength).

Self: The most important element in humor is the ability to laugh at one's self. Set a goal to laugh at one's self at least twice daily for a given period of time (i.e., 30 days), and keep a daily record of your successful investments. You can laugh internally or externally (a smile is mandatory).

Others: (Business) Discuss the importance of humor in the day-to-day functioning of your team. Discuss the difference between laughing "with" others as opposed to laughing "at" them. How important is it that a leader laugh easily at himself or herself? What is the impact of healthy humor on team dynamics? (Family) Discuss how humor can be used to hurt others. Laughing at other people's expense can cause great pain. Humor directed at one's self is mirthful and never causes pain in others. Have family members give real-life examples of both.

Rate Yourself:

1	2	3	4	5

Relatively Weak   Relatively Strong

CHAPTER 7

When Leaders Become Heroes

Between stimulus and response, there is space. In that space is our power to choose our response. In our response lives our growth and freedom.—Viktor Frankl

No one is born a hero. Heroism cannot be gifted, bought, or sold. It is neither coded in the genes nor an inherited predisposition. Heroism has no link to race, religion, social status, income level, gender, age, or nationality. It matters not how smart you are, how well or poorly you did in school, how high your level of achievement.

What, then, *are* the qualifications for being a hero? Is heroism defined by the action taken or by the intent behind the action? Would Chesley "Sully" Sullenberger, the pilot who famously landed a commercial airliner safely on the Hudson River, be considered a hero if his landing had been unsuccessful and all his passengers had died in the crash? Would we still celebrate his heroism? Does heroism require success in the response, or is the noble effort sufficient?

Before answering that question, and how much heroism is or can be tied to training the heroic response, consider these questions, too: Does heroism always involve courage? Was Sully's action courageous – or simply what his training dictated? What would Sully's response need to have been to be deemed "not courageous"? If Sully had been overcome with fear and panic but still somehow managed to land the plane safely, would he still be a hero? Or even *more* of a hero because he had to fight his nerves? To me, perhaps the most fascinating – and important – issue is how we define Sully's heroism. Was it his single act of brilliant flying, bringing a jetliner down on the Hudson, right next to a gigantic population center, with not a single death? ... or was it his devotion to the training, spanning many years, that enabled the heroic act that saved so many lives? Could Sully be considered a hero because he made enormous personal sacrifices to acquire and perfect the skills necessary to do what he did in that one moment, a moment that may never have arrived in just that incredibly dramatic way?

Perhaps the best way to shed further light on this issue is to look at some things that might *dis*qualify a person from being viewed as a hero.

Reflect for a moment on the profiles of action heroes from the worlds of movies, television, children's books, and so on. What would disqualify Superman, Wonder Woman, Batman, Spiderman, Captain America, Ironman, and so forth, from being action heroes? Could they be afraid, shy, unfocused, possess poor time management skills, lack confidence or competitiveness? Absolutely yes. Because fictional action heroes are imperfect. They can – and usually do – possess a variety of *performance* character flaws, while maintaining hero status. Superman (or Clark Kent) is cautious. Iron Man (or Tony Stark) is impetuous. Spiderman (or Peter Parker) is a nerd. None of these are remotely disqualifying traits for a hero.

What *would* unquestionably disqualify them or anyone from being considered a hero are lapses in moral character. Can Superman, Spiderman, or Captain America ever be dishonest, lack integrity, be unfair, unjust, unkind? Can they be fundamentally disrespectful of others, stingy, or arrogant? No. To me, it's critical to note that both qualification for and disqualification from hero status occurs because of moral character, which governs our treatment of others. Could there be greater validation of the importance of moral character? It's the space that reflects who we are when we are our best self, as well as how we want to be remembered after we're gone. The evidence couldn't be clearer. Our treatment of others, and our devotion to the character muscles that support our treatment of others, are at the very core of what it means to be a hero.

WHAT MAKES HEROISM HEROISM?

Heroism is defined more by the intent of the action than the action itself. When the intent transcends self-interest, and is driven by genuine concern for the welfare of others, the action qualifies as heroic regardless of whether the intended outcome was achieved. Like moral character, heroism is not what you achieve, but how. Many citizen-soldiers and military leaders, enshrined in monuments and plaques in town squares in cities across the world, gave their life or led their bat-talions or squadrons in defeat – but did so selflessly and for the right cause (at least as far as their fellow fighters or future commemorators were concerned). If Flight 1549 had crashed into the Hudson River and there were no survivors, Sully's action could still, because of his intent, be considered heroic. There is more to consider, however. If Sully had been drinking or partying the night before, if he had willfully neglected his normal sleep, eating, and performance routines, then the calculus for his heroism would change dramatically. In that case, his intent could still be noble; but if his life choices compromised his fly-ing skills (his response to the crisis), resulting in a crash, he would be immediately disqualified as a hero. Or if Sully had allowed his personal problems to interfere with his ability to avert the crisis, he would be disqualified as a hero; for example, if he was distracted to the point that he failed to follow protocols or was unable to make sound judgments, he would not be looked at as a hero.

What if Flight 1549 had crashed because Sully had not devoted his absolute best – proper energy and time – to acquiring the flying skills and knowledge that ultimately could have saved the day? Sul-ly's adherence to following his optimal pre-performance routines for working out, eating, and sleeping, to his following precise pre-flight mental and emotional routines, to his being fully engaged in his FAA Compliance training and flight training upgrades – were those prereq-uisites for his heroism? Is lack of that adherence an automatic disquali-fier of heroism?

Isn't heroism best understood not as a single visible act but as countless, largely invisible acts that enable the heroic action to become reality?

Considering all the variables, heroism may be best understood not as a single tangible act but as countless, largely invisible acts that enable the heroic action to become reality. Could the heroic action of Ashley Aldridge, a 19-year old mother, who ran barefoot from her home for more than 100 yards to save the life of a complete stranger trapped in a wheelchair between tracks at a railroad crossing, placing herself in grave danger, just materialize by itself? When someone donates a kidney to a stranger to save a life, when a soldier sacrifices his own life to save the lives of his comrades by falling on a live grenade – aren't such examples of extreme altruism enabled by largely invisible, preparatory acts spanning months and even years? Or the majority of a lifetime up to that moment? Could small acts of everyday kindness, everyday acts of patience, caring, and compassion be the real enablers? Our ability to perform heroic acts on behalf of others is essentially a trained response. Consider the doctors, nurses, first responders, essential workers, and others who risked their lives for others during the COVID-19 pandemic. These heroic acts – along with those of military special forces, firefighters, law enforcement officers, and so on – do not just mysteriously happen. These people are doing what their training has prepared them to do: place themselves in harm's way for the benefit of others, for a cause much bigger than themselves. Aren't all these people, in a real sense, *training to be heroes*? Isn't their heroism baked into their devotion to the daily training that makes their heroic act possible?

Character may be manifested in the great moments, but it is made in the small ones.—Winston Churchill

---

Could not your daily journal writing be considered a form of heroic training?

This is why most real heroes are quick to say that they didn't do anything special. They actually mean it. The individual was simply doing what he or she thought was right, simply doing what their training empowered them to do. What we should recognize are the countless selfless acts, largely invisible and unnoticed, that make heroism possible.

TRAINING THE HEROIC RESPONSE

It is in the invisible space between the stimulus and the response that heroism is born. Heroism is uncommon and noble, and because of its rarity and humanity, it is celebrated, often mythologized. A true hero, however, never seeks heroic status. The motivation behind heroism is never a self-enhancing one. The intent is always the same: concern for others. It is a manifestation of a clear shift from the ordinary (a preoccupation with oneself) to the extraordinary (a preoccupation with others).

Consider the following:

1. While at Harvard's Center for Moral Education, renowned developmental psychologist Lawrence Kohlberg developed a six-level theory of moral development. Level 1 begins with morality as a mere consequence of forced obedience and fear of punishment, and proceeds to Level 6, where morality is the result of a highly trained, principled conscience. From his experience and research, Kohlberg believed that only a small percentage of adults would reach a moral level where their lives were governed by higher ethical and moral principles. Level 6, he thought, was rare – but possible.

2. One-third of the participants in Stanley Milgram's experiments on obedience to authority (referenced in Chapter 2) *did* in fact resist the pressure from authority figures and refused to shock the students at levels above 300 volts – not the majority of participants – but a considerable portion.

I take heart in these two examples and countless others. It's clear that something extraordinary can happen between the stimulus and the response, when "ordinary" people produce an extraordinary response on behalf of others – often strangers. Might your daily journal writing be considered a form of heroic training? When you train to be more compassionate, kind, trustworthy, humble, tough-minded, just and fair, are you not training the uncommon response? Are you not demonstrating that uncommon is possible, first in yourself and then in others? Are you becoming heroic without even knowing it?

FROM HEROES IN TRAINING TO HEROES IN WAITING

After a lifetime of studying evil, psychologist Philip Zimbardo is culminating his brilliant career with the creation of what he calls The Heroic Imagination Project. According to Zimbardo, the ultimate goal of this chapter of his life is to increase the occurrence of acts of everyday heroism in society. He intentionally changed his focus from understanding the roots of evil, the dark side of humanity, to understanding and cultivating humankind's capacity for goodness. Zimbardo strongly contends that anyone can be a hero, and that, in fact, everyone can become a "hero in waiting" by taking small steps and nurturing heroic imagination in ourselves and in our children.

How would you feel if, at the end of your life, the person you actually were met the person you could have become?

Living a brilliant purpose brings energy, fulfillment, and well-being to your life.

Living a brilliant character legacy brings energy, fulfillment, and well-being to the lives of others long after you are gone.

Zimbardo's Heroic Imagination Project reminds me of the extraordinary writings of Joseph Campbell, the American mythologist and author of numerous books, including the classic *The Power of Myth*. Campbell spent his professional life exploring common elements of humanity, particularly the stages of the hero-quest. For Campbell, a universal thread in the story of humanity is the endless struggle between good and evil. George Lucas, creator of *Star Wars*, sought advice from Campbell in writing the epic story that would capture the hearts and minds of legions of viewers, young and old. The *Star Wars* story depicts the universal battle of life as one between the forces of good, represented by the Jedi and Yoda, and the forces of evil, represented by Darth Vader, the Stormtroopers, and others. As we develop and become wiser, we recognize that evil dwells not as a force in the external world but within us. Darth Vader, symbol of evil, lies dormant inside each of us, just waiting to be summoned. In reality, the battle is me against myself; Me as my Selfish, Ego-Centered Self versus Me as my Best Moral Self. The hero's journey is a call to align our life more fully with our higher nature, our core values and sense of goodness. When we accept the call, we agree to engage in an often-fierce battle between the forces of weakness and those of strength (our Yoda). The power of Yoda is cultivated through dedicated training and effort. Eventually, if we refuse to surrender, we will slay the inner demon, emerging stronger and more prepared for a life of service to others.

True heroism is remarkably sober, very undramatic. It is not the urge to surpass all others at whatever cost, but the urge to serve others at whatever cost.—Arthur Ashe

Every successful battle is followed by a brief celebratory moment and then suddenly we are awakened, yet again, by another call to heroism, a call to go into battle and slay one more personal demon. As long as we accept the call to confront our moral weaknesses, our hero's journey will continue until our last day.

The main protagonists in the *Star Wars* universe were the Jedi knights, an order devoted to citizenship, acts of charity, and volunteerism. Their mission was always to help and protect those in need, particularly the helpless.

What is the common thread in

- Pausing between the stimulus and the response
- Acts of heroism like Sully's
- Purpose training
- Awareness training
- Character muscle training
- Heroes-in-training
- Heroes-in-waiting
- Jedi knights, and
- Leading with character?

They are all founded on the ideas of treating others the way we want to be treated; putting the welfare of others before our own; making how we treat others in the chase to the top more important than getting to the top.

For leaders, the most important takeaway from this book, I believe, is that we are all vulnerable to lapses in character, with potentially disastrous consequences – yet each of us possesses the power to intentionally convert moral weakness into strength. Although every day we witness good men and women falling from grace, we also witness leaders who refuse to take moral shortcuts, refuse to compromise their character to succeed and win. Daily moral strength-training is a powerful, viable answer. And, as we have explored, by leading with character, we not only help our fellow human beings; we get to know what it is to live a truly successful life. We maximize *our* happiness and sense of well-being. In our treatment of others, we are not just leaving a brilliant legacy for after we are gone; we are creating a brilliant legacy in the here and now.

This book started with Heraclitus's powerfully terse quotation: "Character is destiny." I end with a quotation from the theologian Tryon Edwards: "Thoughts lead on to purposes; purposes go forth in action; actions form habits; habits decide character; and character fixes our destiny."

CHARACTER CALL-OUTS

For You   For Work   For Family

DETERMINATION / PERSISTENCE / GRIT

Definition: The acquired disposition to rally one's strength of will in overcoming obstacles; to refuse to give up (Performance Strength).

Self: The ability to resist quitting at something simply because it becomes difficult or hard is an essential strength in life. Learning to play a musical instrument, learning a new sport that's very challenging, not giving up on trying to reprogram your new watch or installing a new software program on your computer can be repurposed to become strengthening exercises for this character disposition. Read Angela Duckworth's book entitled *Grit*.

Others: (Business) Have each team member describe an example where an important breakthrough was achieved because they were determined not to quit or give up. Discuss how team members can repurpose the obstacles they face daily to strengthen their determination. (Family) Have each family member give two examples each week of where they used their willpower to keep from quitting or giving up at something. Discuss why this character strength is so important to success is life.

Rate Yourself:

1	2	3	4	5
Relatively Weak				Relatively Strong

Character Call-Outs

For You   For Work   For Family

ADVENTUROUS SPIRIT

Definition: The acquired disposition to seek exciting challenges for personal exploration (Performance Strength).

Self: It is possible to awaken every day to the vision that life is a daring adventure but that mindset requires concentrated training to become reality. The fact is life is filled with danger, uncertainty, and risks. To view life in the spirit of the great adventure requires rescripting the tone and content of one's Private Voice until that perception of the world becomes dominant. The best way to do that is to start each day by writing for 5 minutes on "Life as the great adventure." Read what you wrote the previous day and then write a fresh, new message addressing the same theme. Strengthening this muscle will take three to four weeks to start getting the results you want.

Others: (Business) Great leaders inspire their people to see beyond the confusion, uncertainty, risk, and danger. It is in the spirit of adventure that great innovations and breakthroughs become reality. Fear undermines both performance and engagement. Have a different team member each week prepare a written statement and read to team on the topic "My job in the spirit of the great adventure." (Family) Have a family discussion on how seeing life as a great adventure might impact levels of happiness, excitement, and fulfillment in life. Explain that it's possible to view the world in this way but that it takes concentrated training of one's adventure muscle. Give concrete examples of how this performance character muscle can be strengthened. Two of the best strategies are writing and reading.

Rate Yourself:

1	2	3	4	5
Relatively Weak				Relatively Strong

CHARACTER CALL-OUTS

For You   For Work   For Family

TOUGH-MINDEDNESS / MENTAL TOUGHNESS

Definition: The acquired disposition to control one's thoughts; mental strengths of thought and focus (Performance Strength).

Self: The key to tough-mindedness and mental toughness is the ability to control the focus of one's attention. Thought control is an acquired ability and represents the central core of mental toughness. Thought control can be strengthened from any number of common daily activities. Examples would include focusing on eating while eating, on driving while driving, on what others are saying when they're talking, and on what's relevant to winning when playing sports. Anytime thought control is practiced, like meditation, yoga, martial arts, and so forth, the muscle of mental toughness is strengthened.

Others: (Business) The muscles of focus and mental toughness are closely related. Mental toughness is the acquired ability to focus when competitive or performance pressures are intense. Ask team members how tough-mindedness/mental toughness are manifested by team members on a day-to-day basis. Ask for concrete examples. Discuss how leadership and mental toughness are linked. Ask team members to provide practical strategies for building the mental toughness muscle. (Family) Sports, exams, family competitions, and so forth provide excellent training opportunities for strengthening your ability to focus under pressure. Start with no-pressure situations like meditation and yoga, and gradually transition to higher levels of pressure situations. Keep an accurate record of your efforts.

Rate Yourself:

1	2	3	4	5
Relatively Weak				Relatively Strong

CHARACTER CALL-OUTS

For You   For Work   For Family

SEEKING CHALLENGES

Definition: The acquired disposition to constantly look for ways to expand current limits by stepping outside one's comfort zone (Performance Strength).

Self: The complexities of modern life continue to demand more and more from us. To meet those demands, we must continue to expand our limits physically, emotionally, mentally, and spiritually. Growth and expending our limits are nearly synonymous. We expand our physical limits by going to the gym and pushing ourselves beyond our comfort levels aerobically and anaerobically. Climbing mountains, running races, biking cross-country, and so on accomplish the same ends. Challenging ourselves emotionally stimulates growth in the same way. Setting goals that make us more emotionally vulnerable expands our emotional limits. Challenging ourselves mentally to master a new business skill or new language, or challenging ourselves spiritually to acquire a deeper sense of purpose in life broadens our limits. To strengthen your challenge muscle, set goals on a regular basis that push you to discomfort in the area you want to grow. Keep a record.

Others: (Business) Most successful leaders recognize that to survive in business, you've got to continue to grow. Great leaders are constantly challenging their people to learn new things, to take on new responsibilities, to push their limits. High-performance cultures are growth cultures. Growth is hard but deeply fulfilling. The things that push us the most often help us the most. Discuss how seeking new challenges is fundamental to team success. (Family) Family members must challenge themselves to discomfort physically, emotionally, mentally, or spiritually to grow as persons. Have family members report back how they challenged themselves to discomfort during the week.

Rate Yourself:

1	2	3	4	5
Relatively Weak				Relatively Strong

CHARACTER CALL-OUTS

For You   For Work   For Family

OPTIMISM

Definition: The acquired disposition to generate strong belief and faith in a positive future (Performance Strength).

Self: At the end of each day, take one or two of your most concerning issues and re-frame them in an optimistic and hopeful context. Do your reframing in writing for at least 4 to 5 minutes.

Others: (Business) Provide team members with a series of facts about the company's business. Have each prepare two stories from the same facts – one pessimistic and one opportunistic. Discuss relevance to leadership. (Family) Have each family member construct two distinctly different stories from the same five facts. One story provides little hope and is clearly pessimistic, and the other story is hopeful and optimistic. Have each apply to his or her own life.

Rate Yourself:

| 1 | 2 | 3 | 4 | 5 |

Relatively Weak   Relatively Strong

CHARACTER CALL-OUTS

For You   For Work   For Family

CURIOSITY

Definition: The acquired disposition to be inquisitive, to understand how things work (Performance Strength).

Self: At least three times every day, ask yourself the question "I wonder how that works?" Spend a few minutes being curious about what you see. Keep a daily log of your efforts.

Others: (Business) Have team members write for 5 minutes on the role curiosity plays in leadership followed by a discussion of its relevance. Discuss ways to strengthen the curiosity muscle. (Family) Have each family member pick something to be curious about and report back during family meetings. Discuss why curiosity is an important character strength in life.

Rate Yourself:

1	2	3	4	5
Relatively Weak				Relatively Strong

CHARACTER CALL-OUTS

For You   For Work   For Family

ORGANIZATION

Definition: The acquired disposition to be orderly (Performance Strength).

Self: Strengthening this character muscle can be achieved by picking one thing every two weeks to organize. Examples would include cleaning off one's desk before leaving work at night, creating a "things to do" list prior to launching your day, hanging up all your clothes before retiring to bed, and reviewing your calendar of appointments and obligations before the day starts. Whenever you convert disorganization into organization, you stimulate character growth in this area and build momentum towards more organization.

Others: (Business) Read books, take classes, ask for help from people on your team who have exceptional abilities in this area. David Allen's book *Getting Things Done* and his workshops have helped many strengthen their organizational abilities. Devote some energy and time every day to grow this muscle and keep a detailed log of your investments. (Family) Rotate family responsibilities for organizing the chaos of family living. Assignments can last from two weeks to four weeks before the next rotation. Tasks include setting and clearing the table at mealtime, loading the dishwasher, taking out the trash, putting dishes away, putting groceries away, and so on. Individual tasks that are to occur every day with no rotation include things like making one's bed before leaving home, putting toys away, hanging up coats in the closet, and so forth. All these actions help to strengthen organizational competencies.

Rate Yourself:

1	**2**	**3**	**4**	**5**
Relatively Weak				Relatively Strong

ACKNOWLEDGMENTS

The greatest gifts to my character have been my parents, Mary and Con, and my three sons, Michael, Patrick, and Jeffrey. The influence of these five people on the person I have become, ethically and morally, is beyond calculation. Other powerful influences I am immensely grateful for are my brother Tom and sister Jane (Sister Margaret Mary). I continue to be inspired by their depth of character, particularly their kindness and caring for others. To C.J. Loehr for being an extraordinary mother to our three sons.

I want to thank Caren Kenney for her support and devotion to this book and for her help in shaping its content in a significant way. I also want to thank Lowinn Kibbey for encouraging me to write this book and providing me with the time to do so. This book would not have been possible without the support and help of Caren, Lowinn, Andy Postman, and Sandy Friedrich. Sandy's tireless work ethic, her countless sacrifices, and remarkable attention to detail were truly extraordinary.

To Alex Gorsky, Peter Fasolo, Bill Weldon, Sandi Peterson, and Calvin Schmidt for believing in the value we could bring to the world.

To John Collingwood, Kevin Wildenhaus, Chris Jordan, Bill Donovan, and Jenny Susser for their insightful help with the manuscript.

To my co-founder and longtime friend of 25+ years, Dr. Jack Groppel, for his loyal friendship through thick and thin, to his persistent belief and devotion to our business, and to his brilliant ethical and moral character.

To Mary Lauria and Barbara Rodriguez for providing the opportunity to innovate and trial the Character Course, which forms the basis of this book.

To all the current and former Human Performance Institute staff of whom I am so proud, especially Chris Osorio, Bill Donovan, Steve Page, Lorenzo Beltrame, Raquel Garzon, Caroline Rivera, Becky Hoholski, Mike Florence, Greg Lieberman, Kevin Morris, Joy Norton, Sharon Helgerud, Dwayne Wright, Diane Nisbett, Tim Walker, Melissa Scott, Jenn Lea, Brenda Ranero, Chris Allredge, Emily Lewinger, Aileen Teira, Bruce Highfield, Dawn Epstein, Lesandra Hale, Sarah Wallgren, Brian Ballay, Ashley Meyers, Cheryl Branciforte, Kirsten Westlund, and Taisha Ramseur.

To Fred Harburg, Bob Carr, Catherine McCarthy, Jenny Evans, Bill McAlpine, Cindy Heroux, Steve and Jessalynn Bush, Jill Sharp, Jenn George, Stacey Sullivan, Theresa Robinson, Paul Wylie, Lynn Seth, Rhonda Waters, Natalie Johnson, Phil Black, Tara Gidus Collingwood, Greg Grazen, Chris and Kara Mohr, and Phil Burton for their brilliant coaching and facilitation on behalf of our clients.

To so many wonderful J&J employees who have influenced my thinking, especially Len Greer, Jennifer Turgiss, Raphaela O'Day, Shawn Mason, Francine Mitchell, Jennifer Bruno, and Lindsey Brooks.

To all the clients who have touched my life and helped form the basis of my thinking, and to the countless thought leaders and researchers who have inspired this work.

To Tom Gullikson, Coach Guy Gibbs, Kevin Accola, Barbra Schulte, Phebe Farrow-Port, Molly Fletcher, Rick Jacobs, George Dom, Ray Smith, Steve Reinemund, Chip Bergh, A.G. Lafley, Peter Scaturro, Tom Davin, David Leadbetter, Jim and Susanna Courier, Jeanne Ashe, Charlie Kim, Vic Strecher, Dan and Karen Jansen, Paul Roetert, Pat Van der Meer, Jorge Andrew, Julie Jilly, Louie and Helma Cap, Roy Barth, John Evert, Paul Goldstein, Jay Senter, Doug MacCurdy, Renee Heckler, Renate Gaisser, Lee DeYoung, Luis Mediero, Dan Santorum, Emilio Sanchez, Tore and Eddie Rasavage, Anni Miller, John Evans, Maggie Borer, Paul and Kathy Lubbers, Steve Devereux, Randy Gerber, Carey and Helen Bos, Matt Turner, Bill and Mary Rompf, Kevin Kempin, Greg Mason, Amy Wishingrad, Billy Donovan, Brett Ledbetter, Jeff and Sherri Sklar, Cat and Jessica Bradu, Doug Lennick, Ignacio Monsalve, Fritz Nau, Walker and Ray Sahag,

Gloria Caulfield, Virginia Savage, and Miguel Esperanza for your friendship and unwavering support over so many years.

To Pat Loehr, for his creative illustrations.

Finally, and most importantly, to four extraordinary human beings – Vickie Zoellner, Gordon Uehling, Michael Rouse, and Walter Buckley – for continuing to inspire me to pursue my dream.

Appendix A: Character Traits

Every one of these character strengths – either performance strengths (P) or moral strengths (M) – is an acquired disposition.

1. Adaptability: You adjust well to changing conditions (performance strength (P)).
2. Adventurous Spirit: You seek exciting challenges for personal exploration (P).
3. Affection: You openly show warmth and caring toward others (moral strength (M)).
4. Ambition: You are goal-oriented and goal-directed (P).
5. Authenticity: Your Public and Private Voices are aligned; you are genuine (M).
6. Compassion: You feel a deep, abiding concern for the suffering of others, combined with the aspiration to do something to relieve it (M).
7. Competitiveness: You enjoy pitting your skills against the skills of others (P).
8. Confidence: You believe in your abilities (P).
9. Creativity: You generate original, spontaneous thinking and solutions (P).
10. Critical Thinking: You think in a reality-based way (P).
11. Curiosity: You are inquisitive; you want to understand how things work (P).
12. Decisiveness: You make definitive choices (P).
13. Dependability: You can be counted on to meet your commitments (M).

14. Determination/Persistence/Grit: You rally your strength of will to overcome obstacles; you refuse to give up (P).

15. Discernment: You seek the deeper causes of things (P).

16. Empathy: You experience what others are thinking and feeling (M).

17. Engagement with Others: You bring your full and best energy to the present moment in your interactions with others (M).

18. Focus: You can control your attention (P).

19. Forgiveness: You are able to clear the record for those who have harmed you (M).

20. Fortitude: You fight relentlessly for what's right (P).

21. Generosity: You share whatever you have with others (M).

22. Gratitude: You feel sincere appreciation for what you have (M).

23. Honor: Your actions and decisions reflect the highest ethical standards (M).

24. Humility: You are modest and highly aware of your short-comings (M).

25. Humor: You can laugh at yourself and the ironies of life (P).

26. Justice: You are fair in your dealings with others (M).

27. Kindness/Love/Care: You have a deep regard and affection for others (M).

28. Love of Learning: You find joy in discovering new things (P).

29. Loyalty: You are faithful to your friends, family, and associates (M).

30. Moral Courage: You act in accordance with what you believe is right despite any risk or negative consequences to you or to others (M).

31. Moral Integrity: You act in accordance with what you judge to be right (M).

32. Motivation: You energize yourself to act (P).

33. Open-Mindedness: You are receptive to new ideas and thoughts (P).

34. Optimism: You generate strong belief and faith in a positive future (P).

35. Organization: You are orderly (P).

36. Patience: You accept imperfections in others (M).

37. Personal Courage: You act in accordance with what you believe is the right thing to do despite any risks or negative consequences to you (P).

38. Positivity: You view the world through the eyes of opportunity rather than survival (P).

39. Prudence: You exercise good judgment (P).

40. Punctuality: You honor time commitments (P).

41. Resiliency: You bounce back from disappointment or loss (P).

42. Respect: You treat everyone with dignity (M).

43. Seeking Challenges: You constantly look for ways to expand current limits by stepping outside your comfort zone (P).

44. Self-Awareness: You have reality-based perceptions of yourself (P).

45. Self-Control/Willpower: You mobilize the necessary energy to exercise restraint over your impulses, desires, and emotions, and to fulfill your intentions (P).

46. Tough-Mindedness/Mental Toughness: You control your thoughts; you are mentally strong and focused (P).

47. Trust: You believe in the basic goodness of others (M).

48. Truthfulness: You accurately report events and facts as you know them (M).

49. Vitality/Vigor: You feel energetic; you feel enthusiasm for life (P).

50. Wisdom: You formulate insights into the deeper meaning of life (P).

Appendix B: Forces and Factors That May Corrupt Your Moral Reasoning and Judgment

1. The more uncertain and uninformed you are, the more susceptible you are to influence.

2. You are more likely to change beliefs when those beliefs and attitudes are not based on your personal experience.

3. The more informed you are of relevant and necessary facts, the more you can resist outside influence to alter or change your moral thinking and attitudes.

4. Not understanding why you hold certain beliefs makes you more vulnerable to influence.

5. An important distinction must be made between belief and knowledge. Belief is something not immediately susceptible to verification. Knowledge is something based on verifiable facts. Beliefs often masquerade as knowledge.

6. Indoctrination by others is accelerated when you are dependent on the indoctrinator (strong dependency ties) in some way, and when the indoctrinator is able to restrict information flow so that conflicting messages are kept to an absolute minimum.

7. Your need for conformity and obedience can cause you to become an agent in destructive processes.

8. Large breaches in ethics often begin by allowing a very small infraction that doesn't seem to be all that important or serious at the time.

9. Behavior that is inappropriate or unthinkable in your value system may be executed without hesitation when carried out under orders.

10. Your psychological need to be obedient and respect authority can completely override personal ethics and moral conduct.

11. You are much more willing to be part of something that is against your personal ethics if you are only one of many people involved. The ethical dilemma is diminished because the part you play in the overall scheme appears so small.

12. The power of culture to undermine your valued moral code is real and undeniable.

13. When rules have been set that are not consistent with your personal ethics, you have great difficulty disobeying them unless you have considerable peer support.

14. One dissenter is often sufficient for you to reveal your contrary positions.

15. You often change your behavior to achieve social approval. Group pressure to conform can precipitate significant behavior change.

16. When you are part of a crowd witnessing something clearly wrong or unjust, not acting can become the socially acceptable thing to do.

17. When you have committed yourself to a particular position, even though the attachment was not that strong in the first place, all too often you will increase your commitment when your position is attacked or challenged ("boomerang effect").

18. When coerced, you may adopt the very behavior and beliefs forced upon you so you can believe you are in control – that it was *your* choice.

19. You can create justification for holding two inconsistent beliefs by tailoring an expedient story that reduces the cognitive dissonance.

20. The more insecure you are about who you are and what you believe, the more likely it is that you can be persuaded to assume the beliefs of those around you.

21. The more normal a situation is made to appear, the more vulnerable you are to influence and deception. You have no reason to summon your critical voice.

22. Accepting the premise that another person is more powerful, more competent, and more in control than you affords that person greater opportunity for influence.

23. Powerful social forces can be generated for you to align your thinking with the majority to achieve unanimity of thought with those around you. The social force to achieve unanimity can cause you to completely overlook opposing arguments. This often happens in unanimous resolutions in the U.S. Congress.

24. Extreme experience of emotion – such as elation, joy, love, excitement – can make you more susceptible to influence.

25. The illusion of invulnerability serves only to increase the ease with which you can be controlled.

NOTES

CHAPTER 1. WHAT DOES "LEADING WITH CHARACTER" MEAN?

7 Reuters (2009). The Most Destructive Financial Crisis Since the Great Depression (February 27).

12 Segal, S. (2016). Enron Scandal: The Fall of a Wall Street Darling. *Investopedia* (December 2).

12 Tran, M. (2002). WorldCom Accounting Scandal. *The Guardian* (August 9).

12 Brown, K., and Dugan, I.J. (2002). Arthur Andersen's Fall from Grace Is a Sad Tale of Greed and Miscues. *Wall Street Journal* (June 7).

12 Lenzner, R. (2008). Bernie Madoff's $50 Billion Ponzi Scheme. *Forbes* (December 12).

13 36% Increase: Rivera, K., and Karlsson, P. (2017). CEOs Are Getting Fired for Ethical Lapses More Than They Used To. *Harvard Business Review* (June).

Berger, S. (2019). Top Reason CEOs Were Ousted in 2018 Was Because of Scandal. CNBC (May 15, 2019). cnbc.com/2019/05/15/pwc-strategy-report-top-reason-ceos-were-ousted-in-2018-was-scandals.html.

Hinchliffe, E. (2018). CEO Turnover Reached an All-Time High in August. *Fortune* (May). fortune.com/2018/09/12/ceo-turnover-record-high/.

Frangos, C. (2018). 3 Transitions Even the Best Leaders Struggle With. *Harvard Business Review*. hbr.org/2018/07/3-transitions-even-the-best-leaders-struggle-with.

Kwoh, L. (2013). When the CEO Burns Out. *Wall Street Journal* (May 7). wsj.com/articles/SB10001424127887323687604578469124008524696.

14 The distinction between performance character and moral character was first made by Thomas Lickona and Matthew Davidson in a high school character training manual (2005).

16 Ebbers, Etc., All Sent To Prison: Solthes, E. (2016). Why They Do It. *Public Affairs* 1.

18 Volkswagen Scandal: Gates, G., Ewing, J., Russell, K., and Watkins, D. (2017). How Volkswagen's "Defeat Devices" Worked. *New York Times* (March 16).

21 Moral Numbing: Slovic, P. (2007). *Psychic Numbing and Genocide. Psychological Science Agenda*. American Psychological Association (November).

21 Brennerman, R., and Pierson, B. (2017) Blacksands Pacific Executive Charged with $300 Million Fraud. *Reuters* (June 1).

22 Motivated Reasoning: Kunda, Z. (1990). The Case for Motivated Reasoning. *Psychological Bulletin* 108 (3): 480–498.

22 INSYS Therapeutics: Mukherjee, S. (2016). Feds Arrest 6 Former INSYS Execs for Allegedly Bribing Doctors. *Fortune* (December).

22 Ethical Fading: Tenbrunsel, A.E., and Messick, D.M. (2004). The Role of Self-Deception in Unethical Behavior. *Social Justice Research* 17: 223–236. June 2004.

23 Deborah Kelley/Sterne Agee: Raymond, N., and Ingram, D. (2016). NY Pension Fund Manager, Brokers Charged in Pay-to-Play Scheme. *Reuters* (December 21).
Swart, T (2019). Why You Need to Understand the Neuroscience of Imposter Syndrome. *Forbes* (August 8).
Weiss, A., Burgmer, P., and Mussweiler, T. (2018). Two-Faced Morality: Distrust Promotes Divergent Moral Standards for the Self Versus Others. *Personality and Social Psychology Bulletin* 44 (12). researchgate .net/publication/325404027_Two-Faced_Morality_Distrust_Promotes_ Divergent_Moral_Standards_for_the_Self_Versus_Others.

24 Cunyat-Agut, M., Vilar, M.M., and Suay, F. (2016). Moral Reasoning and Decision Making, Brain Structures Involved in Moral Reasoning: A Review. *International Journal of Psychological and Cultural Genomics, Consciousness & Health Research* 2 (2).

25 Ford Pinto Deaths: Bonner, J., Greenleaf, S., and Scarbrough, R. (2011). Ford Pinto Fires Case Study and Executive Summary Essay. *Bartleby Publications* (February 28).

25 Barry Bonds: Bloom, B. (2007). Bonds Indicted on Federal Charges, Federal Grand Jury Indicts Bonds. *MLB.com* (November 16).

25 Dennis Kozlowski's Conviction: White, B. (2005). Ex-Tyco Executives Convicted. *Washington Post* (June 18).

26 Sam Waksal's Conviction: Herper, M. (2003). Sam Waksal Sentenced. *Forbes* (June 10).

26 Bernie Madoff Ponzi Scheme: Lenzner, R. (2008). Bernie Madoff's $50 Billion Ponzi Scheme. *Forbes* (December 12).

26 Ariely, D. (2012). *The (Honest) Truth About Dishonesty*. New York: Harper-Collins: 27.

CHAPTER 2. WHY GOOD LEADERS ARE VULNERABLE TO CORRUPTION: A FLAWED MORALITY SYSTEM

34 Stanley Milgram's Research on Obedience to Authority: Milgram, S. (1963). Behavioral Study of Obedience. *Journal of Abnormal and Social Psychology*: 67 (4); 371–378.

35 Replication of Milgram's Research in Poland: Dolinski, D., Milgram, S., Grzyb, T., Folwarczny, M., Grzbata, P., Krzyszycha, K., Martynowska, K., and Trojanowski, J. (2017). Would You Deliver an Electric Shock in 2015? Obedience in Experimental Paradigm, Developed by Stanley Milgram in the 50 Years Following the Original Studies. *Social Psychological and Personality Science* 8 (8). spsp.org/news-center/press-releases/milgram-poland-obey.

36 Edwin Sutherland Statistics: Sutherland, E. (1949). *White Collar Crime*. New York: The Dryden Press. An excellent review of Sutherland's book was done by Thomas Emerson and published by Yale Law School Legal Scholarship Repository. (1950).

38 *ScienceDaily* (2013). Professional Ethicists Behave No Better . . . Ethicists Behavior Not More Moral (May 21).

38 Integrity Represents 50% of Our Moral Character: This is the author's conclusion after a decade of work in character. Fifty percent is making the right moral decision and 50% is acting on the decision. Without both, morality does not exist.

38 See Eyal, N. (2016). "Have We Been Thinking about Willpower the Wrong Way for 30 Years?" *Harvard Business Review* (November 23). See Strecher, V. (2016). *Life on Purpose: How Living for What Matters Most Changes Everything*. New York: HarperCollins: Chapter 7.

38 More than a quarter: Soltes, E. (2016). *Why They Do It: Inside the Mind of the White-Collar Criminal*. New York: Hachette: 177.

41 Rules of Storytelling: Loehr, J. (2007). *Power of Story* New York: Free Press: 137–139.

41 Your Crap Detector: Loehr, J. (2007). *Power of Story*. New York: Free Press: 117–119.

47 Catholic Priest's Abuse: Hundreds of Priests Shuffled World-Wide Despite Abuse Allegations (2004). USA Today/Associated Press (June 20).

48 Tenbrunsel, A., and Messick, D. (2004). "We Are Creative Narrators," Ethical Fading: The Role of Self-Deception in Unethical Behavior. *Social Justice Research* 17: 225.

48 The Power of Mindset: Dweck, C. (2006). *Mindset: The New Psychology of Success*. New York: Random House.

Ludwig, D., and Longenecker, C. (1993). The Bathsheba Syndrome. *Journal of Business Ethics*. (April).

Solzhenitsyn, A. (1973). The Gulag Archipelago (3 Volumes).

50 Blind Spots: For an excellent review of how our moral calculus can be hijacked and corrupted by bounded awareness, ethical fading, motivated blindness, selective recall, and outcome bias see Bazerman, M., and Tenbrunsel, A. (2011). *Blind Spots*. Princeton, NJ: Princeton University Press.

51 Haidt, J (2001). The Emotional Dog and Its Rational Tail. *Psychological Review*, 108, 814–834.

Kohlberg, L., and Kramer, R. (1969) Continuities and Discontinuities in Childhood and Adult Moral Development. *Human Development* 12:93–120.

Turiel, E. (2006). The Development of Morality. In M. Eisenberg, W. Damon, and R.M. Lerner (Eds.), *Handbook of Child Psychology* (pp. 789–857). Hoboken, NJ: Wiley.

Greene, J. (2001). An fMRI Investigation of Emotional Engagement in Moral Judgment. *Science* 293 (5537): 2105–2108.

(1) Intuitive vs. Cognitive processing systems in human morality. Haidt (2001) emphasizes the role of emotion in moral judgment whereas Kohlberg (1969) and Turiel (2006) emphasize controlled cognition. Joshua Greene and others propose a dual-process morality.

52 (2) System 1 and System 2: This is the language of Daniel Kahneman presented in Kahneman, D. (2011). *Thinking, Fast and Slow*. New York: Farrar, Straus and Giroux. It received the National Academy of Sciences best book award in 2012. System 1 is fast, instinctive, and emotional, while System 2 is slower, more logical, and more deliberative.

54, 59 Joshua Greene is a professor of psychology at Harvard University and director of Harvard's moral cognition lab.

(a) Greene, J. (2013). *Moral Tribes: Emotion, Reason, and the Gap Between Us and Them*. New York: Penguin Press: 353.

(b) Greene, J. (2014). Beyond Point-And-Shoot Morality: Why Cognition (Neuro) Science Matters for Ethics. *Ethics* 124 (4): 695–726. jstor.org/stable/10.1086/675875.

CHAPTER 3. WHO IS THE TRUE ARCHITECT OF OUR CHARACTER?

59 These questions were presented to participants during character courses offered by the Human Performance Institute spanning nearly a decade.

60 The story of evolution is from *Why We Believe What We Believe*, by Andrew Newberg, professor and director of research at the Marcus Institute of Integrative Health.

60 Conscious awareness and morality are inexorably bound together. See King, M., and Carruthers, P. (2012). Moral Responsibility and Consciousness. *Journal of Moral Philosophy* 9: 200–228.

62 Context of multiple: Cognitive neuroscience, rather than using the language of multi-minds, uses constructs such as implicit memory and perception, the continuum of consciousness, mental awareness, preconscious, and nonconscious mental processing. See Kihlstrom, J. (1993). The Continuum of Consciousness. *ScienceDirect* 2 (4): 334–354.

63 The iceberg metaphor is attributed to Freud (1915). He used the language of conscious, preconscious, and unconscious. For Freud, the unconscious mind is the primary source of human behavior. Freud, S. (1915). *The Unconscious*, first published in *Zeitschrift*, vol. 3. Standard Edition 14: 159–204.

63 The "rider and the elephant" metaphor comes from psychologist Jonathan Haidt in his book *The Happiness Hypothesis*.

64 Two Brains: see Pessoa, L. (2009). Cognition and Emotion. *Scholarpedia* 4 (1): 4567. In *The Cognitive–Emotional Brain*, Professor Pessoa argues that brain circuits that constitute the emotional brain influence brain circuits that constitute the cognitive brain and vice-versa. Emotion and cognition are functionally integrated in the brain.

65 Feelings are an integral component of the machinery of reason – Damasio and the orbitofrontal cortex (OFC): Damasio, A.R. (1996). The Somatic Marker Hypothesis and the Possible Functions of the Prefrontal Cortex. *Philosophical Transactions of the Royal Society of London B* 351, 1413–1420. See also Bechara, A., Damasio, H., and Damasio, A. (2000). Emotion, Decision Making, and the Orbitofrontal Cortex. *Cerebral Cortex* 10 (3): 295–307.

66 Much of what we think by our rational brains is driven from our emotional brains: see LeDoux, J. (2015). Feelings: What Are They and How Does the Brain Make Them? *American Academy of Arts and Sciences*. doi:10.1162.

67 The Empathy Circuit: Baron-Cohen, S. (2011). *The Science of Evil: On Empathy and the Origins of Cruelty*. New York: Basic Books: 25–26, 29–45, 153–154, 157, 171 (fig.).

67 According to Kiehl, psychopaths think: See:
(a) Emer, E., Kahn, R., Salovey, P., and Kiehl, K.A. (2012). Emotional Intelligence in Incarcerated Men with Psychopathic Traits. *Journal of Personality and Social Psychology* 103 (1): 194–204.
(b) Kiehl, K.A., Smith, A.M., Hare, R.D., Mendrek, A., Forster, B.B., Brink, J. and Liddle, P.F. (2001). Limbic Abnormalities in Affective

Processing in Criminal Psychopaths as Revealed by Functional Magnetic Resonance Imaging. *Biological Psychiatry* 50: 677–684.

  (c) Ashley Aldridge Act of Heroism: The Carnegie Hero Fund Commission presented Ashley Marie Aldridge the Carnegie medal in 2016, for saving the life of Earl C. Moorman. The act of heroism occurred on September 15, 2015.

68 A common bio-chemical substrate (Oxytocin): See Argiolas, A., Gessa, G. (1991). Central Functions of Oxytocin. *Neuroscience Biobehavioral Reviews* 15 (2): 217–231.

CHAPTER 4. WHO ARE WE BECOMING IN THE CHASE TO THE TOP?

70 "This is the True Job. . .": George Bernard Shaw, Epistle Dedicatory to Arthur Bingham Walkley, Man and Superman; A Comedy and a Philosophy, first published in 1923.

71 The true self has been conceived to be a set of innate: For an excellent review of the True Self construct, see Schlegel, R., and Hicks, J. (2011). The True Self and Psychological Health: Emerging Evidence and Future Directions. *Social and Personality Psychology Compass* 5 (12): 989–1008.

72 is something called: The construct of self-determination has been advanced principally by the research and writings of Ed Deci and Richard Ryan. Deci, E. (1980); Deci, E. and Ryan, R. (1991). Their approach to motivation and personal growth is more aligned with our experience and training approach at HPI.

77 Strecher, V. (2016). *Life on Purpose: How Living for What Matters Most Changes Everything.* New York: HarperCollins. Vic Strecher's book provides the latest research on how purpose interacts with health and happiness.

78 Referred to as Firms of Endearment: Sisodia, R., Wolfe, B., and Sheth, J. (2014). *Firms of Endearment.* Upper Saddle River, NJ: Prentice Hall.

78 called Deliberately Developmental companies: Kegan, R., Lahey, L., Miller, M.L., Fleming, A., and Helsing, D. (2016). *An Everyone Culture: Becoming a Deliberately Developmental Organization.* Boston: Harvard Business Review Press.

78 Beginning with the Greek: Epicurus believed that pleasure is the greatest good. The highest form of pleasure; according to his thinking was a simple, moderate life spent with friends.

78 Aligned with many... Three excellent readings: (1) *Man's Search for Meaning* by Viktor Frankl (1985); (2) *Flourish* by Martin Seligman (2011); and (3) Striving for the Sacred: Personal Goals, Life Meaning, and Religion (2005), by Robert Emmons. *Journal of Social Issues* 61: 731–746.

83 Antagonist muscles, synergistic muscles, prime mover, etc.: Scanlon, V., and Sanders, T. (2015). *Essentials of Anatomy and Physiology*: 154–155.

87 Tendency to be rude: Kleef, G., Homan, A.C., Finkenauer, C., Gündemir, S. and Stamkou, E. (2011). Breaking the Rules to Rise to Power. *Social Psychological and Personality Science* 2 (6). doi:10, 1177.

87 To act sexually inappropriate: Keltner, D. (2016). *The Power Paradox*. New York: Penguin Press: 119–120.

87 To ignore the law: Power Corrupts, but It Doesn't Have To. (2016) *Harvard Business Review*, Interview with Dr. Dacher Kettner, Professor of Psychology at University of California at Berkeley (October 13). hbr.org/ideacast/2016/10/power-corrupts-but-it-doesnt-have-to.

88 To share less: Piff, P., Stancato, D.M., Côté, S., Mendoza-Denton, R., and Keltner, D. (2012). Higher Social Class Predicts Increased Unethical Behavior. *Proceedings of the National Academy of Sciences (PNAS)* 109: 4086–4091.

88 DeCelles, K.A., DeRue, D.S., Margolis, J.D., and Ceranic, T.L. (2012) Does Power Corrupt or Enable? When and Why Power Facilitates Self-Interested Behavior. *Journal of Applied Psychology*: 97 (3): 681–689.

88 In the August 2017 issue of the *Harvard Business Review*: Chamorro-Premuzic, T., and Lusk, D. The Dark Side of Resilience. *Harvard Business Review* (September 14).

119 Levine, E.E., and Schweitzer, M.E. (2014) Are Liars Ethical? On the Tension Between Benevolence and Honesty. *Journal of Experimental Social Psychology*: *Genera* 53: 107–117.

90 Myelin coats the axons of neurons (called myelination) with a fatty coating that provides electrical insulation and strengthens the nervous system. Kirkwood, C., (2015). Myelin: An Overview. *Society for Neuroscience*. brainfacts.org/brain-basics/neuroanatomy/articles/2015/myelin.

93 HPI Tennis Academy Results: 1 player became ranked on the pro tour; 1 Eddie Herr Champion (Junior World Champion); 1 National Champion; 10 State Champions and several runner ups. Players were recruited to play and study at William and Mary; Cornell; West Point; Harvard; University of Pennsylvania; University of Chicago; Samford; Navy; Bowdoin; University of Georgia; Georgia Tech; Rice; Stetson; Clemson and UCF. Many graduates played #1 for their schools and were chosen as captains for their leadership skills.

CHAPTER 5. THE BRICKS AND MORTAR OF CREDO-BUILDING

94 Rand, A. (1982). *Philosophy: Who Needs It.* New York: Bobbs-Merrill Co.: 6.

95 Newberg, A., and Waldman, M. (2006) *Why We Believe What We Believe: Uncovering Our Biological Need for Meaning, Spirituality, and Truth.* New York: Free Press: 5. Newberg is Associate Professor of Radiology and Psychiatry at the University of Pennsylvania. Waldman is Associate Fellow at the Center for Spirituality and the Mind at the University of Pennsylvania.

96 As early as 2002: Moll, J., de Olivera-Souza, R., Bramati, I.E., and Grafman, J. (2002). Functional Networks in Emotional Moral and Non-Moral Social Judgments. *Neuroimage* 16 (3, Part 1): 696–703.

100 Corporate Social Responsibility: For an excellent overview of the Life and Legacy of Robert Wood Johnson, see Foster, L.G. (2008) *Robert Wood Johnson and His Credo: A Living Legacy.* Lillian Press.

104 Cadet Honor Code: Is a formalized written statement of the minimum standard of ethics expected of cadets. Any cadet accused of violating the code faces an investigative and hearing process. usma.edu/scpme/SitePages/Honor.aspx.

105 Seal Code: A Warrior Creed. navyseals.com/nsw/seal-code-warrior-creed/.

107 For the two best sources for Mintzberg's insights on managerial practices, see Mintzberg, H. (1973). *The Nature of Managerial Work.* New York: Harper & Row; and Mintzberg, H. (1990) The Manager's Job: Folklore and Fact. *Harvard Business Review* (March–April).

114 in the form of writing: Journaling has been a central component of HPI's programs for over 20 years. We draw on the research in three areas: narrative psychology, expressive writing, and spaced repetition. The following research articles are representative: Pennebaker, J. (1997). Writing about Emotional Experiences as a Therapeutic Process. *Psychological Science* 8 (3): 162–166; Smyth, J., and Lepore, S. (2002). The Writing Cure: How Expressive Writing Promotes Health and Emotional Well-being. *American Psychological Association*; Kang, S. (2016). Spaced Repetition Promotes Efficient and Effective Learning: Policy Implications for Instructing. *Behavioral and Brain Sciences* 3 (1): 12–19.

CHAPTER 6. EMBEDDING YOUR PERSONAL CREDO AND SUPPORTING IT WITH HABITS

127 "If I always appear prepared, it is because. . .": Napoleon Bonaparte, French general, politician, and emperor (1769–1821). Retrieved from Spiewak, P. (2006). *Do You Want to Be a Leader?* Trafford Publishing. https://books.google.com/books?id=x0lFp9ks09gC&pg=PA64&lpg =PA64&dq=if+i+always+appear+prepared,+it+is+because%E2%80% A6%E2%80%9D:+napoleon+bonaparte,+french+general,+politicia n,+and+emperor&source=bl&ots=XGTEv98OOU&sig=ACfU3U0 vPZnXNDlIm0R7dVwnTlFocv4SDQ&hl=en&sa=X&ved=2ahUK Ewi62OqwvpbqAhVOmXIEHSbuAOcQ6AEwAHoECBAQAQ#v=- onepage&q=if%20i%20always%20appear%20prepared%2C%20it%20 is%20because%E2%80%A6%E2%80%9D%3A%20napoleon%20 bonaparte%2C%20french%20general%2C%20politician%2C%20 and%20emperor&f=false.

128 25-second period between points: Loehr, J. (1990). *The Mental Game.* New York: Penguin: 105–112.

129 Ideal Performance State: Loehr, J. (1986). *Mental Toughness Training for Sports.* New York: Penguin: 22–35.

130 The key to building: Loehr, J. (2012). *The Only Way to Win.* New York: Hyperion: 103–110.

131 Lowel, S., and Singer, W. (1992). The Selection of Intrinsic Horizontal Connections in the Visual Cortex by Correlated Neuronal Activity. *Science* 255. See also Hebb, D. (1949). *The Organization of Behavior: A Neuropsychological Theory.* New York: Wiley.

134 PTR^3 is consistent with Charles Duhigg's approach to habit building described in Duhigg, C. (2012). *The Power of Habit.* New York: Random House. The words he uses to explain a habit loop are "cue," "routine," and "reward."

CHAPTER 7. WHEN LEADERS BECOME HEROES

154 between stimulus and response: Frankl has been quoted as having written this but it does not appear in either of his books, *Man's Search for Meaning* or *The Doctor and the Soul.* Several authors, including Stephen R. Covey, have reported finding this quote in other non-specific sources.

154 Would Chesley Sullenberger: Rivera, R. (2009) A Pilot Becomes a Hero Years in the Making. *New York Times* (January 17). nytimes .com/2009/01/17/nyregion/17pilot.html.

155 Lawrence Kohlberg developed: Kohlberg, L. (1981). *Essays on Moral Development*, Volume 1: *The Philosophy of Moral Development*. New York: Harper & Row.

160 One-third of the participants: Milgram, S. (1974). *Obedience to Authority: An Experimental View*. New York: HarperCollins.

161 The Heroic Imagination Project: Zimbardo, P. (2007). *The Lucifer Effect: Understanding How Good People Turn Evil*. New York: Random House. The Heroic Imagination Project. heroicimagination.org/.

162 The Heroes' Journey: Campbell, J. (1949) *The Hero with a Thousand Faces*. Princeton, NJ: Princeton University Press.

REFERENCES AND RELATED READINGS

Adams, J.S., Tashchian, A., and Shore, T.H. (2001). Codes of Ethics as Signals for Ethical Behavior. *Journal of Business Ethics* 29: 199–211.

Akers, R.L. (1991). Self-Control as a General Theory of Crime. *Journal of Quantitative Criminology* 7: 201–211.

Apicella, C.L., Carré, J.M., and Dreber, A. (2015). Testosterone and Economic Risk Taking: A Review. *Adaptive Human Behavior and Physiology* 1: 358–385.

Ariely, D. (2012). *The Honest Truth About Dishonesty: How We Lie to Everyone—Especially Ourselves*. New York: HarperCollins.

Arnulf, J., and Gottschalk, P. (2013). Heroic Leaders as White-Collar Criminals: An Empirical Study. *Journal of Investigative Psychology and Offender Profiling* 10: 96–113.

Balcetis, E., and Dunning, D. (2006). See What You Want to See: Motivational Influences on Visual Perception. *Journal of Personality and Social Psychology* 91: 612–625.

Bargh, J. A., and Chartrand, T. L. (1999). The Unbearable Automaticity of Being. *American Psychologist* 54: 462–479.

Baron-Cohen, S. (2011). *The Science of Evil*. New York: Basic Books.

Batson, C.D. (1990). How Social an Animal? The Human Capacity for Caring. *American Psychologist* 45: 336–346.

Baumgartner, T., Heinrichs, M., Vonlanthen, A., Fishbacher, U., and Fehre, E. (2008). Kindness and Other Prosocial Acts Such as Empathy and Compassion Are Associated with Elevated Levels of the Hormone Oxytocin. *Neuron* 58 (4): 639–650.

Baumhart, R. C. (1961). How Ethical Are Businessmen? *Harvard Business Review (July–August)* 7–19, 156–176.

Baumeister, R.F., and Tierney, J. (2011). *Willpower: Rediscovering the Greatest Human Strength*. New York: Penguin Press.

Bazerman, M.H., and Tenbrunsel, A.E. (2011). *Blind Spots: Why We Fail to Do What's Right and What to Do About It*. Princeton, NJ: Princeton University Press.

Bazerman, M.H., Tenbrunsel, A.E., and Wade-Benzoni, K. (1998). Negotiating with Yourself and Losing: Making Decisions with Competing Internal Preferences. *Academy of Management Review* 23: 2, 225–241.

Bechara, A., Damasio, A.R., Damasio, H., and Anderson, S.W. (1994). Insensitivity to Future Consequences Following Damage to Human Prefrontal Cortex. *Cognition* 50: 7–15.

Bersoff, D. (1999). Why Good People Sometimes Do Bad Things: Motivated Reasoning and Unethical Behavior. *Personality and Social Psychology Bulletin* 25: 28–39.

Campbell, J. (1991). *The Power of Myth*. New York: Anchor Books.

Chamorro-Premuzic, T., and Lusk, D. (2017). The Dark Side of Resilience. *Harvard Business Review* (August 16), hbr.org/2017/08/the-dark-side-of-resilience.

Clegg, S.R., Kornberger, M., and Rhodes, C. (2007). Business Ethics as Practice. *British Journal of Management* 18 (2): 107–122.

Covey, S.M.R. (2006). *Speed of Trust*. New York: Free Press.

Cueva, C., Roberts, R. E., Spencer, T., Rani, N., Tempest, M., Tobler, P. N., Herbert, J., and Rustichini, A. (2015). Cortisol and Testosterone Increase Financial Risk Taking and May Destabilize Markets. *Scientific Reports* 5: 1–16.

Das, G. (2009). *The Difficulty of Being Good*. New York: Oxford University Press.

DeCelles, K.A., DeRue, D.S., Margolis, J.D., and Ceranic, T.L. (2012). Does Power Corrupt or Enable? When and Why Power Facilitates Self-Interested Behavior. *Journal of Applied Psychology* 7: 681–689.

Decety, J., Michalska, K.J., and Kinzler, K.D. (2011). The Developmental Neuroscience of Moral Sensitivity. *Emotion Review* 3: 305–307.

Deci, E.L. (1980). *The Psychology of Self-Determination*. Lexington, MA: Lexington Books, D.C. Heath.

de Waal, F. (1996). *Good Natured: The Origins of Right and Wrong in Humans and Other Animals*. Cambridge, MA: Harvard University Press.

de Waal, F. (2006). *Primates and Philosophers: How Morality Evolved*. Princeton, NJ: Princeton University Press.

Duckworth, A. (2016). *Grit: The Power of Passion and Perseverance*. New York: Simon & Schuster.

Elm, D.R., and Nichols, M.L. (1993). An Investigation of the Moral Reasoning of Managers. *Journal of Business Ethics* 12: 817–833.

Emer, E., Kahn, R., Salovey, P., and Kiehl, K.A. (2012). Emotional Intelligence in Incarcerated men with Psychopathic Traits. *Journal of Personality and Social Psychology* 103(1): 194–204.

Eyal, N. (2016). Have We Been Thinking about Willpower the Wrong Way for 30 Years? *Harvard Business Review* (November 23).

Fanelli, D. (2009). How Many Scientists Fabricate and Falsify Research? A Systematic Review and Meta-Analysis of Survey Data, *PLOS|One*, doi: 10.1371/journal.pone.0005738.

Flack, J.C., and de Waal, F. (2000). Being Nice Is Not a Building Block of Morality. *Journal of Consciousness Studies* 7:67–78.

Forte, A. (2004). Antecedents of Managers' Moral Reasoning. *Journal of Business Ethics* 51: 315–347.

Gailliot, M.T., and Baumeister, R.F. (2007). The Physiology of Willpower: Linking Blood Glucose to Self-Control. *Personality and Social Psychology Review* 11 (4): 303–327.

Gellerman, S. W. (1986). Why "Good" Managers Make Bad Ethical Choices. *Harvard Business Review* (July-August): 85–90.

Gino, F. (2015). Understanding Ordinary Unethical Behavior Why People Who Value Morality Act Immorally. *Behavioral Sciences* 3: 107–111.

Gino, F., and Ariely, D. (2012). The Dark Side of Creativity: Original Thinkers Can Be More Dishonest. *Journal of Personality and Social Psychology* 102: 445–459.

Gino, F., and Galinsky, A.D. (2012). Vicarious Dishonesty: When Psychological Closeness Creates Distance from One's Moral Compass. *Organizational Behavior and Human Decision Processes* 119: 15–26.

Gino, F., Schweitzer, M.E., Mead, N.L., and Ariely, D. (2011). Unable to Resist Temptation: How Self-Control Depletion Promotes Unethical Behavior. *Organizational Behavior and Human Decision Processes* 115: 191–203.

Gladwell, M. (2005). *Blink: The Power of Thinking without Thinking*. Boston: Little, Brown.

Goleman, D. (1998). *Working with Emotional Intelligence*. New York: Bantam.

Graham, J., and Haidt, J. (2010). Liberals and Conservatives Rely on Different Sets of Moral Foundations. *Journal of Personality and Social Psychology* 96: 1029–1046.

Graham, J., Nosek, B.A., Haidt, J., Iyer, R., Koleva, S., and Ditto, P.H. (2011). Mapping the Moral Domain. *Journal of Personality and Social Psychology*: 101, 366–385.

Grant, A. (2014). *Give and Take*. New York: Penguin Books.

Greene, J. (2013). *Moral Tribes: Emotion, Reason, and the Gap Between Us and Them*. New York: Penguin Press.

Hagger, M.S., Wood, C., Stiff, C., and Chatzisarantis, N.L.D. (2010). Ego Depletion and the Strength Model of Self-Control: A Meta-Analysis. *Psychological Bulletin* 136: 495–525.

Haidt, J. (2012). *The Righteous Mind: Why Good People Are Divided by Politics and Religion*. New York: Pantheon.

Hauser, M. (2006). *Moral Minds: How Nature Designed Our Universal Sense of Right and Wrong*. Ecco.

Hogeveen, J., Inzlicht, M., and Obhi, S.S. (2014). Power Changes How the Brain Responds to Others. *Journal of Experimental Psychology: General* 143: 755–762.

Huebner, B., Dwyer, S., and Hauser, M. (2009). The Role of Emotion in Moral Psychology. *Trends in Cognitive Sciences* 13: 1–6.

Josephson Institute. (2008). Report Card on the Ethics of American Youth, charactercounts.org/programs/reportcard/.

Kabat-Zinn, J. (1994). *Wherever You Go, There You Are: Mindfulness Meditation in Everyday Life*. New York: Hyperion.

Kegan, R., Lahey, L., and Laskow, L. (2016). *An Everyone Culture: Becoming a Deliberately Developmental Organization*. Boston: Harvard Business Review Press.

Keltner, D., and Haidt, J. (2003). Approaching Awe, a Moral, Spiritual, and Aesthetic Emotion. *Cognition and Emotion* 17: 297, 314.

Kern, M., and Chugh, D. (2009). Bounded Ethicality: The Perils of Loss Framing. *Psychological Science* 20: 378–384.

Kiehl, K.A., Smith, A.M., Hare, R.D., Forster, B.B., Brink, J., and Liddle, P.F. (2001). Limbic Abnormalities in Affective Processing in Criminal Psychopaths as Revealed by Functional Magnetic Resonance Imaging. *Biological Psychiatry* 50 (9): 677–684.

Kilburg, R. (2012). *Virtuous Leaders: Strategy, Character, and Influence in the 21st Century*. Washington, DC: American Psychological Association.

Kornberger, M., and Brown, A.D. (2007). Ethics as a Discursive Resource for Identity Work. *Human Relations*: 60 (3): 497–518.

Lang, J. (2013). How College Classes Encourage Cheating, *Boston Globe* (August 6).

Lee, J.J., Gino, F., Jim, E.S., Rice, L.K., and Josephs, R.A. (2015). Hormones and Ethics: Understanding the Biological Basis of Unethical Conduct. *Journal of Experimental Psychology: General* 144: 891–897.

Lennick, D., and Kiel, F. (2007). *Moral Intelligence: Enhancing Business Performance and Leadership Success*. Pearson Education, Wharton School Publishing.

Levine, E.E., and Schweitzer, M.E. (2014). Are Liars Ethical? On the Tension Between Benevolence and Honesty. *Journal of Experimental Social Psychology* 53: 107–117.

Liao, M. (2016). *Moral Brains: The Neuroscience of Morality*. Oxford University Press.

Loehr, J. (1982). *Mental Toughness Training for Sports: Achieving Athletic Excellence*. New York: Plume.

Loehr, J. (1990). *The Mental Game*. New York: Penguin Books.

Loehr, J. (2012). *The Only Way to Win: How Building Character Drives Higher Achievement and Greater Fulfillment in Business and Life*. New York: Hyperion.

Martin, K.D., Cullen, J.B., Johnson, J.L., and Parboteeah, K.P. (2007). Deciding to Bribe: A Cross-Level Analysis of Firm and Home Country Influences on Bribery Activity. *Academy of Management Journal* 50 (6): 1401–1422.

McLean, B., and Elkind, P. (2004). *The Smartest Guys in the Room: The Amazing Rise and Scandalous Fall of Enron*. New York: Penguin.

McGonigal, K. (2008). The Science of Willpower. *IDEA Fitness Journal* (June), ideafit.com/fitness-library/science-willpower-0.

Mead, N.L., Baumeister, R.F., Gino, F., Schweitzer, M.E., and Ariely, D. (2009). Too Tired to Tell the Truth: Self-Control Resource Depletion and Dishonesty. *Journal of Experimental Social Psychology* 45: 594–597.

Mearsheimer, J. (2011). *Why Leaders Lie: The Truth about Lying in International Politics*. Oxford: Oxford University Press.

Merritt, A.C., Effron, D.A., and Monin, B. (2010). Moral Self-Licensing: When Being Good Frees Us to Be Bad. *Social and Personality Psychology Compass* 5: 344–357.

Millar, C.C.J.M., Delves, R., and Harris, P. (2010). Ethical and Unethical Leadership: Double Vision? *Journal of Public Affairs* 10 (3): 109–120.

Moll, J., de Oliveira-Souza, R., Bramati, I.E., and Grafman, J. (2002). Functional Networks in Emotional Moral and Non-Moral Social Judgments. *Neuroimage* 16 (3, Part 1): 696–703.

O'Kelly: E. (2005). *Chasing Daylight: How My Forthcoming Death Transformed My Life*. New York: McGraw-Hill.

Park, N., Peterson, C., and Seligman, M. (2004). Strengths of Character and Well-Being. *Journal of Social and Clinical Psychology* 23 (5): 603–619.

Paxton, J. M., Ungar, L., and Greene, J.D. (2011). Reflection and Reasoning in Moral Judgment. *Cognitive Science* 36: 163–177.

Perez-Pena, R. (2012). Studies Find More Students Cheating, with High Achievers No Exception. *New York Times* (September 7).

Pinto, J.T., Leana, C.R., and Pil, F.K. (2008). Corrupt Organizations or Organization of Corrupt Individuals? Two Types of Organization-Level Corruption. *Academy of Management Review* 33 (3): 685–709.

Ramirez, E. (2008). Cheating on the Rise among High School Students. *US News and World Report* (December 2).

Ruedy, N.E., Moore, C., Gino, F., and Schweitzer, M.E. (2013). The Cheater's High: The Unexpected Affective Benefits of Unethical Behavior. *Journal of Personality and Social Psychology* 105: 531–548.

Seligman, M. (2011). *Flourish: A Visionary New Understanding of Happiness and Well-Being*. New York: Nicholas Brealey Publishers.

Shalvi, S., Gino, F., Barkan, R., and Ayal, S. (2015). Self-Serving Justifications: Doing Wrong and Feeling Moral. *Current Directions in Psychological Science* 24: 125–130.

Shaw, G.B. (1923). Epistle Dedicatory to Arthur Bingham Walkley. In *Man and Superman: A Comedy and a Philosophy*. Reprinted New York: Penguin Classics.

Sims, R.R., and Brinkmann, J. (2003). Enron Ethics (or: Culture Matters More than Codes). *Journal of Business Ethics*, 45 (3) 243–256.

Sisodia: R., Wolfe, B., and Sheth, J. (2014). *Firms of Endearment*. Upper Saddle River, NJ: Prentice-Hall.

Smith, A. (2014). *The Theory of Moral Sentiments*. Excercere Cerebrum Publications.

Smith, N.C., Simpson, S.S., and Huang, C. (2007). Why Managers Fail to Do the Right Thing: An Empirical Study of Unethical and Illegal Conduct. *Business Ethics Quarterly* 17: 633–667.

Strecher, V. (2016). *Life on Purpose: How Living for What Matters Most Changes Everything*. New York: HarperCollins.

Sutherland, E. (1949). *White Collar Crime*. New York: The Dryden Press.

Tenbrunsel, A.E., Diekmann, K.A., Wade-Benzoni, K.A., and Bazerman, M.H. (2011). Why We Aren't as Ethical as We Think We Are: A Temporal Explanation. In *Research in Organizational Behavior*, ed. Staw, B. M., and Brief, A., forthcoming.

Tenbrunsel, A.E., and Messick, D.M. (1999). Sanctioning Systems, Decision Frames, and Cooperation. *Administrative Science Quarterly* 44: 684–707.

Tenbrunsel, A.E., and Messick, D.M. (2004). Ethical Fading: The Role of Self-Deception in Unethical Behavior. *Social Justice Research* 17: 223–236.

Tenbrunsel, A.E., and Smith-Crowe, K. (2008). Ethical Decision Making: Where We've Been and Where We're Going. *Academy of Management Annals* 2: 545–607.

Trevino: L.K., and Youngblood, S.A. (1990). Bad Apples in Bad Barrels: A Causal Analysis of Ethical Decision-Making Behavior. *Journal of Applied Psychology* 75: 378–385.

Vardi, Y. (2001). The Effects of Organizational and Ethical Climates on Misconduct at Work. *Journal of Business Ethics* 29 (4): 325–337.

Vaughan, D. (1999). The Dark Side of Organizations: Mistake, Misconduct and Disaster. *Annual Review of Sociology* 25: 271–305.

Waller, J. (2007). *Becoming Evil*. Oxford: Oxford University Press.

Warren, D., Gaspar, J., and Laufer, W. (2014). Is Formal Ethics Training Merely Cosmetic? A Study of Ethics Training and Ethical Organizational Culture. *Business Ethics Quarterly* 24: 85–117.

Whitacre, M. (2014). When Good Leaders Lose Their Way. *Loyola University Chicago Law Journal* 45: 525–536.

Index

193